Football's "Combo" Defensive System

RHOD REAVES

PARKER PUBLISHING COMPANY, INC.
West Nyack, N.Y.

Dedication

*To my wife, Ruth, for being an understanding
Coach's widow, and the Mother of our three
cheerleaders: Lieschen, Melinda, and Robin.*

© 1977 *by*
Parker Publishing Company, Inc.

West Nyack, N.Y.

Library of Congress Cataloging in Publication Data

Reaves, Rhod
    Football's "combo" defensive system.

    Includes index.
    1. Football--Defense. 2. Football coaching.
I. Title.
GV951.18.R4   796.33'22   77-8862
ISBN 0-13-324152-1

Also by the Author

The Multiple Power I Offense

ADVANTAGES OF THE "COMBO" DEFENSE

This defense blends a combination of sets and techniques from the Stack 44, Split 44, and Eagle 53 defenses. The result of these combinations is a single defensive system with the characteristics of the Pro 43 defense. It is simple and flexible for your players to learn, and it can be adjusted to work successfully against all of the current offensive systems.

This book is for coaches at all levels. This defense can be simplified and adapted to the many offenses that can be encountered from one week to the next at the high school level, without creating new learning situations for your players. It is flexible enough to apply against the current Slot "I," wishbone, and veer offenses. It is also sophisticated enough to handle the pro offensive sets.

As coaches we are constantly aware that tactical offensive innovations dictate changes in the defense. Defenses have always been based on two general characteristics: They either shoot the gaps to prevent hesitation, or they apply techniques to get control before their reaction. Because of offensive false keys and tactical influences, the current trend is to stunt through the gaps of responsibility. The "Combo" system applies both characteristics. Our defensive techniques are based on the theory that most any player with a desire to play football can learn to tackle with a minimum amount of teaching. The reasons most players miss tackles are because of hesitation and being caught out of position. The techniques used in the Combo system create responsibilities for reacting without hesitation and getting into position to make the tackle. There are occasions when tackling drills are necessary as a learning device, so long as they do not discourage tackling or cause unnecessary injuries.

This book presents the application of the "Combo" defensive system against all of the commonly used offenses. You should be able to find the tactical adjustments you need to prepare for any offense. Here are the set adjustments against the slots, flankers, pro-sets, unbalanced lines, double wings, and spreads. This book reveals how to prepare your defenses against the winged T's, slot I's, wishbones, veers, double wings, single wings, and spreads. By use of your own initiative you will be able to add the responsibilities from one chapter to the set of adjustments of another to find the total defense that you might need.

The "Combo" defensive system is the integration of the sets and techniques from a number of the current defenses. Since the offense determines the change in the defense, the "Combo" is flexible enough to change with times in the framework of the system. This is a step-by-step explanation of that system.

Rhod Reaves

The Author's Acknowledgement

I appreciate the strong influences of my late Father, Vic Reaves, who was a very successful football coach for 38 years. I am indebted to John Moore, our former Athletic Director, for the opportunities that he gave me.

Two of our former coaches made many contributions to the "combo" defensive system. They were: Kin Lavender, who was our defensive coordinator, and Bill Green, who was our defensive secondary coach. Since we used strictly a two platoon program, my direct associations were with the offense where I was called the "Rod Father." Our defense had their own saying. It was: "Lavender, Green, Dilly-Dilly." Their reference was to me as being dilly-dilly. Because of the loyalty and cooperation of these two coaches, our program was a very large and close knit family. It was a loss to the profession when these two men left education to enter the business world.

We all three are in agreement that it was a privilege and thrill to have had the opportunity to coach the many fine young men that we had at Ritenour. We had a large number of boys who made good high school players, yet we produced very few of the so called blue chippers as did most of our opponents. We won; and on a number of occasions our teams carried us far beyond the expectations of the coaching staff. This is a tribute to those boys who did not have the natural ability to become college stars, but will become sure winners in the game of life.

Finally, I wish to thank Mrs. Naomi Campbell for doing all of the typing.

CONTENTS

1

THE ORIGIN OF
COMBINATIONS

The combo defensive system is the integration of characteristics and techniques from a variation of many different styles of defenses. It combines techniques to get control, and stunts to get positions based on offensive tactics and personnel tendencies. Our approach to defense is to systematically attack the offense. The 44 stack has had the following influences on our combo defensive system.

ORIGIN OF THE STACK 44 DEFENSE

The stack 44 is an outgrowth of the "Bama" 62 defense. This Alabama defense was popular during the early 60's. It numbered gaps in the same way the offense numbered holes, and then attacked the offense based on calls. This has had a lot of influence on our approach to defense.

FIGURE 1-1 Shows a simplified version of the "Bama" system. It was an eight man front with six down linemen and two linebackers. There were two separate units with each having a guard, a tackle, an end, and a

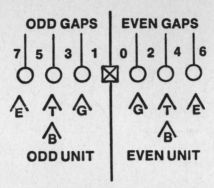

Figure 1-1
The "Bama" 62 System

linebacker. The odd unit was to the left, and the even unit was to the right. They could make separate gap calls independently of one another, and left the defense with four on three men. The six down linemen blocked the men on them before filling the gaps of their responsibilities. This kept the offensive linemen off the linebackers allowing them to get in position to make tackles.

The techniques of the down linemen were to actually block the linemen on them in their numbers and get control, before sliding into the gaps for which they were responsible.

FIGURE 1-2 Shows the basic inside and outside techniques. If the gap called was to his inside he used the outside technique, and if the gap called was to his outside he used the inside technique. The linebacker was responsible for the gap called before his pursuit. This influenced the combo techniques.

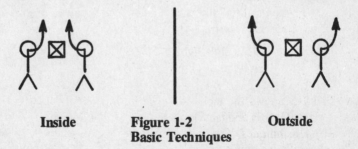

Inside   **Figure 1-2**   Outside
                          Basic Techniques

FIGURE 1-3 Shows the center calls with a "1 gap" to the left and the "O gap" to the right. All down linemen used the outside techniques and the linebackers were responsible for the center gaps. This influenced our interior stacks.

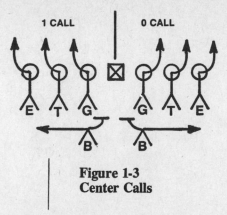

Figure 1-3
Center Calls

FIGURE 1-4 Shows the guard calls with "3 gap" to the left and "2 gap" to the right. Guards used the inside techniques, and tackles and ends used the outside techniques. The linebackers were responsible for the guard gaps. This influenced over 53 sets and techniques after the alignment was moved over center.

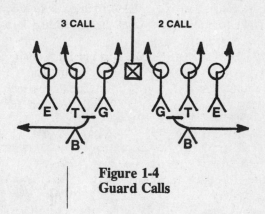

Figure 1-4
Guard Calls

FIGURE 1-5 Shows the tackle calls with "5 gap" to the left and "4 call" to the right. Guards and tackles used the inside techniques and the ends used the outside techniques. The linebackers were responsible for the outside gaps. This also influenced our 53 sets and techniques after the alignment was moved over center.

FIGURE 1-6 Shows the end calls with "7 gap" to the left and "6 gap" to the right. All down linemen applied the inside techniques and the linebackers were responsible for the outside. This influenced our goal line and short yardage defenses.

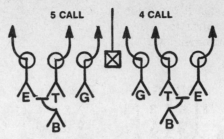

Figure 1-5
Tackle Calls

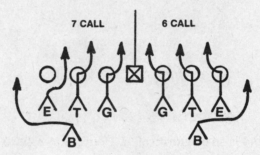

Figure 1-6
End Calls

The offenses caught up with the 62 defense by exploiting its weaknesses. They split the defense, attacked the flanks, and passed to the flats. This forced the defense to shift to a 44 stack set. The walkaway ends stacked their tackles, and the linebackers stacked their guards. This put the defensive front positioned four on three across the line, and the defense applied the same numbering system to attack the offense. The defense had to change their techniques to direct gap stunt calls, because of the three soft spots their sets left across the line. This prevented the offense from splitting the defense, and passing to the flat with consistency.

FIGURE 1-7 Shows the variation of possible stunt calls. It can pressure the offense, and force it to be inconsistent. When the offense does break a play loose it's usually for a big gain, and the defensive sideline can have problems in determining who was responsible. Even though the offense might have out guessed the stunt, you know they are going to try again anything that worked. If the defense does not know where their breakdown was and get it corrected, it will happen again. We have seen a good offensive team get off only two or three successful plays against this defense, but they were for touchdowns. Though it can cause an offense to be inconsistent, it can be inconsistent itself over the long haul. This has influenced our "combo" system only to their split ends' side.

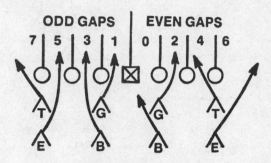

Figure 1-7
44 Stack System

ORIGIN OF THE SPLIT 44 DEFENSE

The split 44 is an outgrowth of the Notre Dame split 62 defense. Its set broke down offensive interior blocking rules, and put emphasis on technique and control to gain position. FIGURE 1-8 Shows the basic split 62 defense.

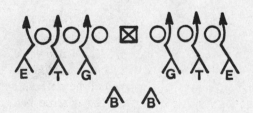

Figure 1-8
Notre Dame 62

The offenses also caught up with this defense by exploiting the same flanker and flat weaknesses. This forced the defense to a split 44 set along with a wide tackle 62 techniques to the outside. FIGURE 1-9 shows the split 44 defense. It features the bump and recover techniques by the outside linebackers, and the split techniques of the inside linebackers who are protected from the offensive guard behind the techniques applied by their tackles. This has influenced, our "combo" defense to the tight end's side.

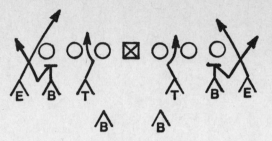

Figure 1-9
Split 44 Defense

ORIGIN OF THE 53 DEFENSE

We needed to integrate an odd set into our combo system without disturbing the sets and techniques of our ends, cornerbacks and secondary. Moving one of our linebackers to a down middle guard and stacking the other linebacker behind him enabled us to achieve this. If we could not find personnel who could handle the different techniques at both positions, then we would substitute. FIGURE 1-10 shows the Eagle 53 defense that influenced the "combo" system's odd interior sets and techniques. We could not have done this with the set of the still popular Oklahoma 52 front.

Figure 1-10
Eagle 53 Defense

There are other reasons why we stayed away from an Oklahoma interior set. Its original purpose was so the interior linebackers could key the guards and immediately react to their movement. Now many linebackers key offensive backs rather than offensive guards. This eliminates their false keys. This has left them exposed and less effective than they once were. FIGURE 1-11 shows a simple scheme that is very effective against linebackers keying guards. It presents a series with a total of 12 plays that could be run behind one blocking scheme, and they could all be called at the line of scrimmage

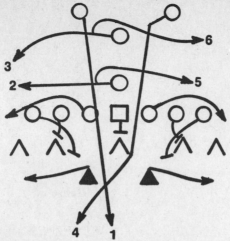

Figure 1-11
False Key Sequence vs. Oklahoma Front

without a huddle. The guards pull deep as they would on a sweep and lead the options. The center blocks straight on and the tackles block out. The tight ends pull behind their tackles and seal where the linebacker is, or was.

The running sequence is:

1. Hand-off to their half back to the left.
2. Fake the hand-off and keep on the option.
3. Fake the hand-off and pitch on the option.
4. Fake the hand-off, and counter hand-off on reverse pivots.
5. Fake the hand-off and keep on the option after the reverse pivots.
6. Fake the hand-off and pitch on the option after the reverse pivots.

Running this sequence to both sides is a total of 12 plays, and the whole line is still blocking the same. If you have not seen this sequence before studying it should leave second thoughts for both defensive and offensive coaches.

COMBINING THE SETS AND TECHNIQUES

Combining these sets and techniques into one "combo" system results in a defense with Pro 43 characteristics. We can have five down linemen with two or three linebackers. We can have four down linemen with three or four linebackers. We can use three or four deep in the secondary. This is integrated into one easy to teach system. It can be adjusted from week to week against different styles of offenses without creating new learning situations for our players. Next comes the positions and set adjustments for the development of the "combo" system.

2

DEVELOPING THE "COMBO" SYSTEM

The "combo" defense is usually a combination of the stack and split 44 defenses along with an Eagle 53 shifted down one half of a man. This is because most offenses have a tight end to one side and a split end to the other. This results in our making our set adjustments based on the set of their tight end. After this is done our other means for set adjustments are based on calls.

SET ADJUSTMENTS BASED ON THEIR TIGHT END

The side to which their tight end is set is called the tight side, and the side away from him is called the split side. The defense must be able to quickly recognize this in order to adjust. The offensive tight sides will have three tight adjacent linemen to one side of center, and the offensive split sides will only have two tight adjacent linemen to the other side of center.

FIGURE 2-1   shows a slot set with the split side to the left and the tight side to the right.

FIGURE 2-2   shows a pro set with the tight side to the left, and the split side to the right.

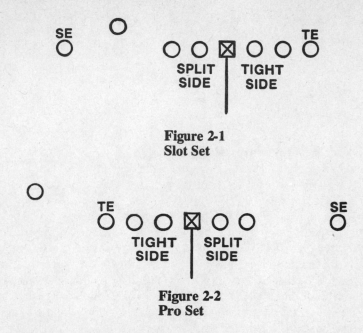

Figure 2-1
Slot Set

Figure 2-2
Pro Set

FIGURE 2-3 shows a tight set with two tight ends and two tight sides.

FIGURE 2-4 shows a split set with two split ends and two tight sides.

FIGURE 2-5 shows an unbalanced set with the tight side to the left, and the split side to the right.

Note: The split end is to the tight side.

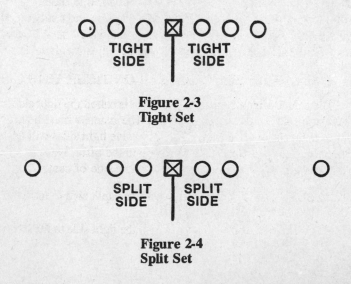

Figure 2-3
Tight Set

Figure 2-4
Split Set

Figure 2-5
Unbalanced Set

All our defensive positions adjust their sets based on offensive split or tight side alignments. This must be done before the snap so assignments——based on calls—can be executed without being caught out of defensive pre-snap positions.

It is important to note here what the big pre-snap differences are between the offense and defense. The offense has the advantages of knowing what they are going to do before the snap and will execute on sound. The defense must react to sight and movement instead of sound. The offense must be set one full second before the snap. The defense must make their set adjustments and have their mental concentration on their assigned responsibilities before the snap. If a defense is going to attack an offense, it must be in a position to execute without hesitation after the snap.

HOW 44 AND 53 DEFENSES ARE ALIKE AND DIFFERENT

The "combo" defense has exterior and interior positions. The seven exterior positions are: the two ends, tight cornerback, split cornerback, safety, and two halfbacks. The four interior positions are: the two tackles, combo, and middle linebacker. The seven exterior positions have the same assignments regardless of the defensive calls. They carry out their responsibilities from their pre-snap set adjustments. The four interior positions must first make their calls for their assignments, and then adjust to the offensive alignments. The following exterior assignments show how all our defenses are the same:
FIGURE 2-6 shows exterior set adjustments for each position to offensive alignments:

Ends (left and right): Both ends are set in three point stances one yard to the outside of either the offensive tight end or split side tackle, and face through them. FIGURE 2-6a shows a slot set with the left end set outside the offensive split side tackle, and the right end set outside the the offensive tight end. FIGURE 2-6b shows a pro set with the left end set outside the offensive tight end, and the right end set outside the offensive split side tackle.

Tight Cornerback is set in a very low two point stance head on the tight end. He flip-flops to the tight side, or with the tight end. FIGURE 2-6a shows

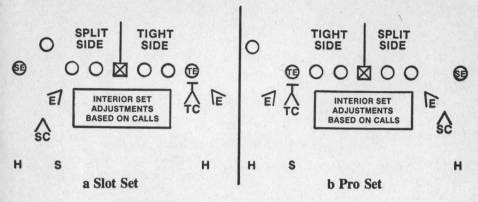

Figure 2-6
Exterior Adjustments to Offensive Line Sets

a slot set with the tight cornerback set on this tight end to the right. FIGURE 2-6b shows a pro set with the tight cornerback set his tight end to the left.

Split Cornerback is in a two-point stance in a walk away position to the split side. He flip-flops to the split side and triangles the split if it is not too wide. FIGURE 2-6a shows a slot set with the split cornerback set in the triangle of their left split. FIGURE 2-6b shows a pro set with the split corner back set in the triangle of their right split.

Safety is set in a two point stance 5 to 7 yards off of the middle receiver. FIGURE 2-6a shows their flanker set in a slot to the left, and is the middle receiver. FIGURE 2-6b shows a pro set with their tight end set to the left and is the middle receiver.

Halfbacks (left and right): Both halfbacks are set in two point stances 8 to 10 yards off the outside shoulders of the outside receivers. 2-6A shows a slot set with their split and tight ends being the outside receivers. 2-6B shows a pro set with their flanker back and split end being the outside receivers.

This places all seven exterior players in proper position before the snap to carry out their responsibilities regardless of which defense is called. The two basic calls we use are "44" and "53." They determine the alignments of the four interior defensive positions. "44" calls are usually applied on passing downs and "53" calls are usually applied on running downs. After these alignments are called they must adjust their positions to the set of the offense.

INTERIOR SET ADJUSTMENTS FOR A "44" CALL

With a "44" call we basically use a stack 44 defensive set to the offensive split side, and a split 44 defensive set to the offensive tight side.

FIGURE 2-7 SHOWS THE FOLLOWING VARIATIONS FOR EACH INTERIOR POSITION IN THEIR 44 SET ADJUSTMENTS:

Figure 2-7A is the set adjustments for a 44 call when their offensive tight side is to the left, and their offensive split side is to the right.

LEFT TACKLE is set in a three point stance to the inside shoulder of his offensive left tackle.

COMBO is set in a two point stance off the line of scrimmage over his offensive left guard

RIGHT TACKLE is set in a three point stance on his offensive right guard.

MIDDLE LINEBACKER is set in a two point stance stacked behind his defensive right tackle.

Figure 2-7B is the set adjustments for a 44 call when their offensive split side is to the left and their offensive tight side is to the right.

LEFT TACKLE is set in a three point stance on his offensive left guard.

COMBO is set in a two point stance stacked behind his defensive left tackle.

RIGHT TACKLE is set in a three point stance to the inside shoulder of his right offensive tackle.

MIDDLE LINEBACKER is set in a two point stance off the line-of-scrimmage over his offensive right guard.

Figure 2-7C is the set adjustments for a 44 call when there are two offensive tight sides.

TACKLES (left and right) are both in three point stances to the inside shoulders of their respective offensive guards.

COMBO AND MIDDLE LINEBACKER are both in two point stances off the line of scrimmage over their respective offensive guards.

Figure 2-7D is the set adjustments for a 44 call when there are two offensive split sides.

TACKLES (left and right) are both in three point stances set on their respective offensive guards.

COMBO AND MIDDLE LINEBACKER are both in two point stances stacked behind their respective defensive tackles.

The 44 calls are our even defenses. If we need to change to an odd defense we will make a "53" call.

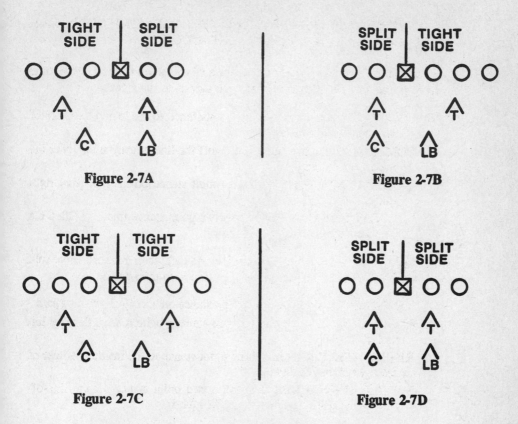

Figure 2-7A

Figure 2-7B

Figure 2-7C

Figure 2-7D

Interior Set Adjustments to a 44 Call

INTERIOR SET ADJUSTMENTS FOR A "53" CALL

With a "53" call we usually apply an Eagle "53" defensive set shifted down toward the tight side of the offense one half of a man.

FIGURE 2-8 SHOWS THE FOLLOWING VARIATIONS FOR EACH INTERIOR POSITION IN THEIR 53 SET ADJUSTMENTS:

Figure 2-8A is the set adjustments for a "53" call when their offensive tight side is to the left, and their offensive split side is to the right.

LEFT TACKLE-is set in a three point stance on his offensive left tackle.

COMBO-is set in a four point stance in the gap between the offensive center and their tightside left guard.

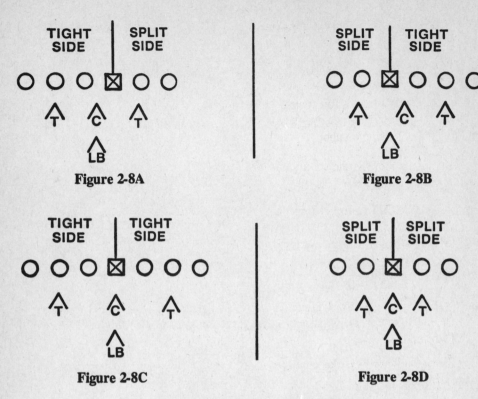

Figure 2-8A

Figure 2-8B

Figure 2-8C

Figure 2-8D

Interior Set Adjustments to a 53 Call

RIGHT TACKLE-is set in a three point stance on his offensive right
guard.

MIDDLE LINEBACKER is in a two point stance off the line-of-
scrimmage over their offensive center.

Figure 2-8B is the set adjustments for a "53" call when their offensive
split side is to the left, and their offensive tight side is to the right.

LEFT TACKLE is set in a three point stance on his offensive left guard.

COMBO is set in a four point stance in the gap between the offensive
center and their tight side right guard.

RIGHT TACKLE is set in a three point stance on his offensive right
tackle.

MIDDLE LINEBACKER is in a two point stance off the line-of-
scrimmage on their offensive center.

Figure 2-8C is the set adjustments for a "53" call when there are two offensive tight sides.

TACKLES (left and right) are both in three point stances set on their respective offensive tackles.

COMBO is in a four point stance on the offensive center.

MIDDLE LINEBACKER is in a two point stance stacked behind his defensive combo.

Figure 2-8D is the set adjustments for a "53" call when there are two offensive split sides.

TACKLES (left and right) are both in three point stances set on their respective offensive guards.

COMBO is in a four point stance on the offensive center.

MIDDLE LINEBACKER is in a two point stance stacked behind his defensive combo.

Now that we have completed all the individual sets adjustment for the "Combo" system, we will apply team alignment against a variation of offensive formations.

APPLYING TEAM SETS TO A VARIATION OF OFFENSIVE FORMATIONS

A variation of "Combo" alignments presents multiple looks against different offensive formations. The currently common offensive formations are the pro-sets and the slot I.

FIGURES 2-9 and 2-10 show the "Combo" team sets applied against these formations:

Figure 2-9 is a 44 "combo" adjustment against a pro set left. It results in split 44 alignment to the left side, and a stack 44 alignment to the right side.

Figure 2-10 is a "53 combo" adjustment against slot "I" set left. It results in a 53 alignment shifted away from the slot. It puts both the split cornerback and safety covering the split side.

After you have studied this "Combo" system you can test your understanding of the rules for team sets by diagraming the correct defensive alignments against some uncommon or unusual offensive formations presented in Figure 2-11. After you have done this you can check yourself with the corresponding answers diagramed in Figure 2-12. Please keep in mind that this is strictly tactical and academic. After scouting reports and statistics reveal the

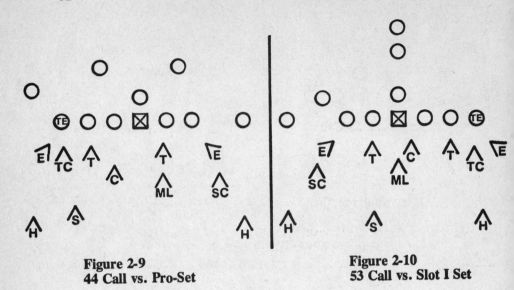

Figure 2-9
44 Call vs. Pro-Set

Figure 2-10
53 Call vs. Slot I Set

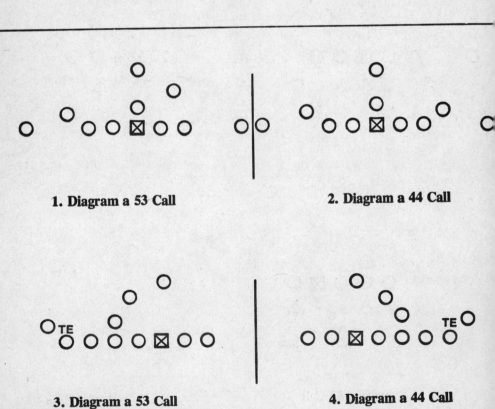

1. Diagram a 53 Call

2. Diagram a 44 Call

3. Diagram a 53 Call

4. Diagram a 44 Call

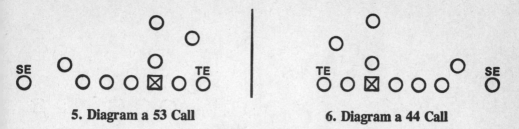

5. Diagram a 53 Call   **6. Diagram a 44 Call**

Figure 2-11
Test for Defensive Sets

After Studying This System, Test Your Understanding
by Diagraming on a Piece of Paper the Defensive Alignments for the Above Offensive Formations. Corresponding Answers are Given in Figure 2-12.

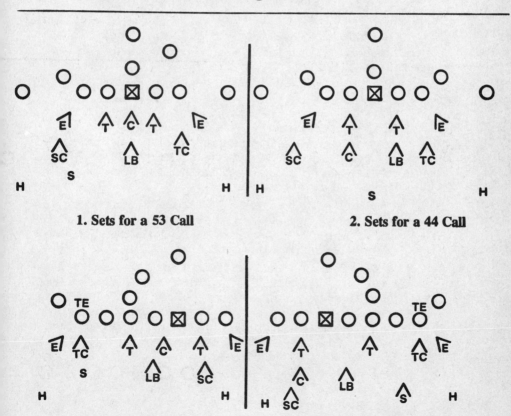

1. Sets for a 53 Call   **2. Sets for a 44 Call**

3. Sets for a 53 Call   **4. Sets for a 44 Call**

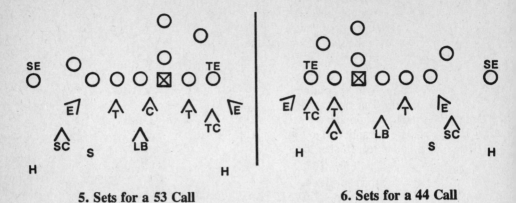

5. Sets for a 53 Call   6. Sets for a 44 Call

Figure 2-12
Corresponding Answers to Test for Defensive Sets

team and personnel tendencies, additional adjustments may be required. As an example, it might be necessary to shift a 44 defense either down a half or full man against an unbalanced line.

FIGURE 2-12 shows the following answers that are diagramed along with an explanation for the respective test in Figure 2-11:

1. Shows a 53 defensive alignment diagramed against a floater slot offensive formation with two split sides. Since there is no defensive tight end the major question should have been what to do with the defensive tight cornerback. He is free, and could be used in the same manner as a rover or Monster.

2. Shows a 44 defensive alignment diagramed against a double-wing slot formation. Again there is no tight end, but he is not free. He must either be substituted by another split cornerback, or take on those responsibilities outside his normal functions.

3. Shows a 53 defensive alignment diagramed against an unbalanced single wing set to our left. This places the tight side to the left and the split side to the right without a split end. Our tight cornerback sets to the left since it is the tight side and he can carry out his normal function on their offensive tight end. As a result the split cornerback has no split end, and is free to serve as a free safety or in invert rotation from the right split side.

4. Shows a 44 defensive alignment diagramed against an unbalanced single wing set to our right. This places the split side to the left without a split end, and the tight side to the right. Our tight corner-back sets to the right since it is the tight side and he can carry out his

normal functions on their offensive tight end. Again the split cornerback has no split end and is free to serve as a free safety or in invert rotation from the left split side.

5. Shows a 53 defensive alignment diagramed against an unbalanced slot "T" formation set to our left. This places the tight side to the left along with a split end, and the split side to the right without a split end. Our tight cornerback sets to the right since their tight end is now positioned on the split side. The split cornerback must triangle the split end to the left tight side, and the safety joins him to cover the left flanker slot.

6. Shows a 44 defensive alignment diagramed against an unbalanced slot "T" formation set to our right. This places the tight side to the right along with a split end, and the split side to the left without a split end. Our tight cornerback sets to the left since their tight end is now positioned on the split side. The split cornerback must triangle the split end to the right tight side, and the safety joins him to cover the right flanker slot.

This completes the means of adjusting the pre-snap alignments for our "combo" defense. This is the base for the system since it puts each individual player in a combination of positions so he will be able to execute his assignments after snap. In order to execute we must have techniques to get control, and then positions of responsibility to make tackles. We have sometimes called our system the 74 combo defense, but this is misleading to the outside. They think in terms of seven down and four up. There are two other reasons why we think in terms of "74." We have already discussed our seven exterior and four interior positions. The other reason is that we basically have seven men on our defensive front who should think run first and pass second. We basically have four men in our defensive secondary who should think pass first, and run second. The following two chapters are the techniques and responsibilities for the post-snap execution of our defensive front and secondary.

3

TEACHING THE RESPONSIBILITIES AND TECHNIQUES OF THE DEFENSIVE "COMBO" FRONT

The seven positions on the defensive front who should think run first are: the two ends, two tackles, combo, middle linebacker, and tight cornerback. The safety, two halfbacks, and split cornerback are the four remaining secondary positions that should think pass first.

DEFENSIVE END PLAY

The ends are to force the running plays and rush the pass. They should make it sheer suicide for a quarterback to keep on an option, forcing him to pitch quickly. If the pitch can be forced before the running back gets to a position beyond his offensive end, the defense should have no trouble with their outside containment. The ends try to get to a position with their inside shoulders between the quarterback and the place where he is trying to pitch to his running back. This position is usually about two yards behind the pre-snap set of the offensive tackle. If the quarterback rolls deep the end maintains his inside shoulder pursuit angle from that position of advantage he gained after the snap.

The technique is a fast take-off on the snap, going through the set of the offensive tackle or tight end. The ends are the only players on the defensive front with basic techniques that do not require defensive control of an offensive position before reacting to carry out their assignments. Their basic techniques have the characteristics of a stunt to quickly get to a position of advantage prior to their reactions to the play.

FIGURE 3-1 Shows the ends forcing the run. The left end forces the quarterback to change his direction, while the right end begins his inside shoulder pursuit from the position he had gained behind their offensive tackles set.

FIGURE 3-2 shows the outside rush applied on a pass pocket.

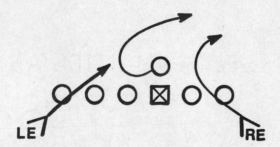

Figure 3-1
Defensive End Play - Force Run

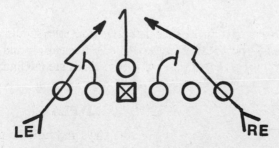

Figure 3-2
Defensive End Play - Rush Pass

DEFENSIVE TACKLE PLAY

The tackles' techniques and responsibilities will vary with their tight or split side alignments, and their 44 or 53 calls. Their responsibilities are what determines the variations, while the techniques they apply are basically the same. They get control on an offensive lineman before carrying out their assigned responsibilities. This control is achieved by making contact in their opponent's numbers with a forearm shiver.

FIGURE 3-3 shows the responsibilities and techniques for a 44 call vs. tight side alignments. Their responsibilities are the gaps between the offensive guard and tackles, and to keep the offensive guards from getting to their

TIGHT SIDES

Figure 3-3
44 Calls vs. Tight Sides

SPLIT SIDES

Figure 3-4
44 Calls vs. Split Sides

TIGHT SIDES

Figure 3-5
53 Calls vs. Tight Sides

SPLIT SIDES

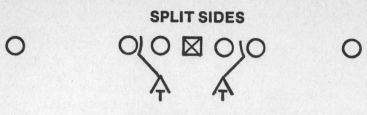

Figure 3-6
53 Calls vs. Split Sides

interior linebackers. They shade the inside shoulders of the offensive tackles before the snap. After the snap they apply a reach technique with a forearm shiver on the offensive guard's outside shoulders, and gain positions of control for their assigned gaps. If their offensive tackles take pre-snap splits that are too big, then the defensive tackles will shoot the gaps.

FIGURE 3-4 shows the tackles' responsibilities and techniques for a 44 call vs. split side alignments. Their responsibilities are the two gaps on both outsides of the offensive guards. They set on the offensive guards before the snap. After the snap they apply a head on technique with forearm shivers and react to pressure after gaining control. They can fill the gaps to the opposite side that the offensive guard will try to slide their heads after contact.

FIGURE 3-5 shows the tackles' responsibilities and techniques for a 53 call vs. tight side alignments. Their responsibilities are the gaps between the offensive tackles and guards, and to keep the offensive tackles off the middle linebacker. They are on the offensive tackles before the snap. After the snap they apply a head on technique with forearm shivers to get a position of control before sliding into the gaps of their responsibilities.

FIGURE 3-6 shows the tackles' responsibilities and techniques for a 53 call vs. split side alignments. Their responsibilities are for the gaps between the offensive guards and tackles, and to keep the offensive tackles off of the middle linebacker. They shade the outside shoulders of the offensive guards before the snap. After the snap they apply a reach technique with a forearm shiver on the offensive tackles' inside shoulders, and gain a position of control for their assigned gaps.

Though our tackles apply basically the same technique to gain positions of control for four different assignments of responsibilities, they present the offense with multiple looks and problems because of the many variations in offensive tight or split side alignments.

THE COMBO PLAY

The combo has the dual role of a middle guard and an interior linebacker.

This doubles his learning situation because of the differences in the characteristics of these two positions. Try to find a player whose talents would suit him to first play middle guard, and then be able to transfer his abilities to linebacker play. It is probably easier to find this type of player at a high school than a college level. If you can't find a player that can naturally adapt to these dual learning situations, then you will have to substitute with two players depending on the situation. We have successfully done it both ways.

FIGURE 3-7 shows the combo's responsibilities and techniques of the dual learning situations based on a 44 and a 53 call.

FIGURE 3-7a: On 44 calls the combo is the left interior linebacker. His responsibilities are to play the football on running plays, and cover the left hook area on pass plays. His techniques are to read the backs through the guards on the left tight side, and to use the protection of his stack on the left split side.

FIGURES 3-7b: On 53 calls the combo is the down middle guard. He sets on the offensive center when there are either two tight sides, or two split sides. His responsibilities are both gaps between the center and the two guards. His technique is to apply a head-on forearm shiver to neutralize the center and maintain control, sliding to either side against pressure by reading the head.

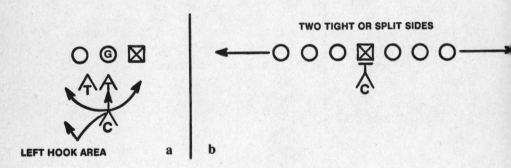

a   b

Figure 3-7
Combo Play

FIGURE 3-8 shows the combo's responsibilities and techniques against a tight side and split side alignment with a 53 call. When the tight side is to the left, the combo sets between the left guard and center and shoots the gap. When the tight side is to the right, the combo sets between the center and right guard and shoots the gap.

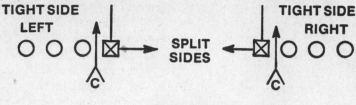

Figure 3-8
53 Combo Play

MIDDLE LINEBACKER PLAY

The middle linebacker's responsibilities are to play the football on running plays, and cover the hook areas on pass plays. 44 and 53 calls determine his alignment before the snap, in order for him to carry out these responsibilities.

FIGURE 3-9 shows the 44 call to the left (Figure 3-9a), and the 53 call to the right (Figure 3-9b). On a 44 call the middle linebacker is the right interior

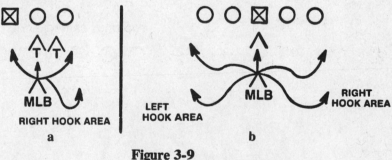

Figure 3-9
Middle Linebacker Play

linebacker. His responsibilities are to play the football on running plays, and cover the right hook area on pass plays. His techniques are to read the backs through the guards on the right tight side, and to use the protection of his stack on the right split side. On a 43 call the middle linebacker stacks the combo, (middle guard), and reads the quarterback through center. He covers the hook area to the side of the offensive backfield flow, and usually covers the left hook area on a straight dropback pass.

TIGHT CORNERBACK PLAY

The tight cornerback flip-flops with the tight side alignment, or set of the offensive tight end. On both 44 and 53 calls, the responsibilities of the tight cornerback is to neutralize the tight end by throwing him off balance, and destroying his timing, before reacting to the play of the football. The technique that he applies is called the "bump and recovery." He used a forearm shiver from a very low two point stance to raise the tight end straight up, and forces him to the outside gaining a position of control to the inside. After a quick look to his inside for the ball carrier, he begins to retreat with the tight end, while looking up field for the play of the football. Once the cornerback finds the football he reacts. The delay as a result of recovery prevents overreaction and being caught out of position. The time used in the "bump and recovery" technique leaves the cornerback in good position to come up and make the play.

FIGURE 3-10 shows the "bump and recovery" technique being applied to both the left and the right tight sides. If there should be two tight ends on the offensive line the split cornerback will have to either be able to share these responsibilities and techniques, or be substituted by another tight cornerback.

There is no reason to ever be penalized for defensive holding or pass interference as a result of the "bump and recovery" technique, because one good blow is all that is necessary to be effective. It destroys the timing in both blocking for running plays and pass pattern, and usually leaves a defensive player in a strategic area that is normally cleared out. We believe that this technique has a harassing effect on the offense.

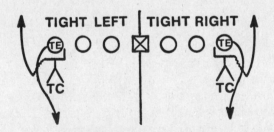

Figure 3-10
Tight Cornerback Play

SPLIT CORNERBACK PLAY

The split cornerback flip-flops with the split side alignment, or set of the offensive split end. On both 44 and 53 calls, he triangles the split and keys

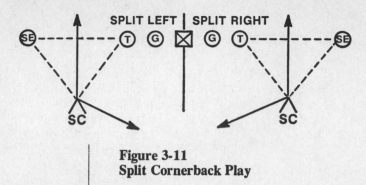

Figure 3-11
Split Cornerback Play

first offensive back to his side out of the backfield. His responsibilities in theory are to think pass first; but in reality, or actual application, he probably thinks run first. He comes up fast if the offensive flow comes to him, and he shares invert reaction with the safety if the offensive flow goes the other way.

FIGURE 3-11 shows the split cornerback's sets in a triangle of the split sides to both the left and the right. It shows the paths of his reactions to the flow of the offensive backfield.

This completes the basic techniques and responsibilities for the combo defensive front. This defensive front is basically a technique defense which gets control and contains. The only penetration of the line-of-scrimmage to force the backfield has been from our defensive ends. A technique defense requires a lot of practice and related drills, and is usually very consistent. It makes the players very conscientious of their responsibilities. It is very basic and dependable, and this is good.

What happens on those occasions when an offense begins to move ball consistently on the defense? Our techniques are breaking down and the defensive front is getting whipped on the line-of-scrimmage. As a result there is hesitation in our reactions. The defense has to change, penetrate, force, and actually attack the offense. This is done with our "combo" stunt system which will be covered in Chapter 5. We number our defensive gaps the same way the offense numbers the holes, and then attack gaps based on calls. Before we get into stunts we need next to cover the basic assignments of our defensive secondary to complete the basic techniques and responsibilities applied in the "combo" defensive system. We have to perfect the basics before we can stunt. We cannot learn to play sound defense beginning with stunts.

4

COACHING THE RESPONSIBILITIES AND TECHNIQUES OF THE DEFENSIVE "COMBO" SECONDARY

The four positions in our deep defensive secondary who should think pass first are: the two half backs, safety, and split cornerback. The tight cornerback, combo, and middle linebacker also have major responsibilities in our pass coverage.

SECONDARY ZONES

Our defensive secondary is divided into five zones. Three of the zones are the deep 1/3s of the field, and two of the zones are the left and right short areas.

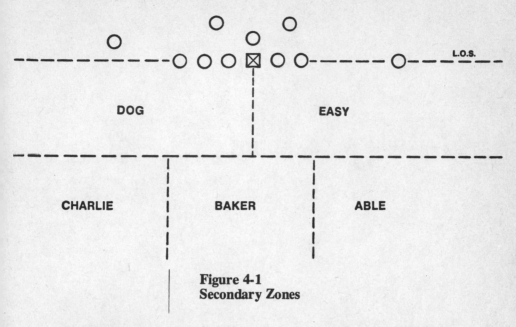

Figure 4-1
Secondary Zones

FIGURE 4-1 shows the names of these zones running clockwise. Able is the right deep 1/3, Baker is the middle deep 1/3, and Charlie is the left deep 1/3. Dog is the short left zone and Easy is the short right zone. These two short zones are basically divided into two parts. There are interior hook areas, and exterior flats. The names of these zones will be used in reference from this point on.

There are basically two kinds of pass coverage. They are zone and man-to-man. There are times when we use zone coverage, and there are other times when we need man-to-man coverage. There are also occasions when the situation calls for applying a combination of both.

ZONE PASS COVERAGE

Zone pass defense has players assigned in designated areas and the responsibility of the coverage of any pass receivers who enter them. It is the best coverage against the bomb, and usually produces the highest percentage of interceptions. A zone is a must if the offense has faster and taller receivers in matching them up man-to-man against our pass defenders. Its weakness is that the zones may be split by fast deployment of pass receivers between the zones. There are difficulties in maintaining zone coverage against double wing and some slot formations.

We use 3 deep with our zone coverage. The right half is responsibile for Able, the safety is responsible for Baker, and the left half is responsible for

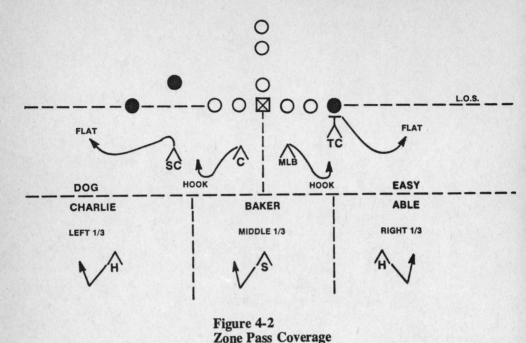

Figure 4-2
Zone Pass Coverage

Charlie. The combo covers the left hook area in Dog, and the middle linebacker covers the right hook area in Easy. The two corner backs cover the exterior flats in Dog and Easy. A 44 defensive call is necessary for complete zone coverage. One of the hook areas will be left uncovered with a 53 call.

FIGURE 4-2 shows zone coverage being applied against a slot set to our left. The split cornerback covers the exterior flat in Dog, and the right cornerback covers the exterior flat in Easy. If the offensive tight side had been to our left the tight cornerback would cover the set in Dog, and if the offensive split side had been to our right then the split cornerback would cover the set in Easy.

MAN-TO-MAN PASS COVERAGE

Man-to-man pass defense is the simplest to understand, and is the most fundamental and tactically sound. If we can match the speed and size of the offensive pass receivers man for man with our pass defenders then we can release the entire defensive front to concentrate on the offensive running plays. The pass defenders can also come up and set much closer to the pre-snap sets of the pass receivers. The weaknesses of man-to-man pass coverage is that there are less pass interceptions, and more dangers of getting a "bomb" thrown deep behind the secondary defenders. Man-to-man pass coverage can be applied with a 44 defensive call, but we basically use it with our 53 defensive calls.

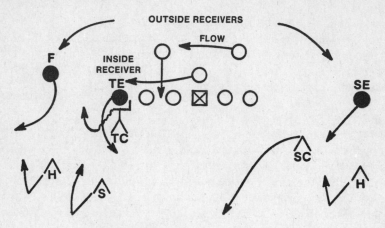

Figure 4-3
Man-to-Man Pass Coverage vs. Pro Set

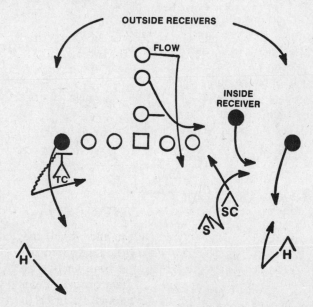

Figure 4-4
Man-To-Man vs. Slot Set

With man-to-man coverage the two halfbacks cover the two outside pass receivers, and the safety takes the inside receiver. The cornerbacks (tight and split) pick up the first running back to their side to come out of the deep backfield.

FIGURE 4-3 shows man-to-man pass coverage vs. a pro set to our left. The flanker back is the outside receiver to our left covered by the left half, and the split end is the outside receiver to the right covered by the right half. The tight end is the inside (middle) receiver covered by the safety. Since the tight end is double covered by the tight corner back and safety, and the offensive backfield flow is to the tight side, the split cornerback is free for invert rotation to Baker.

FIGURE 4-4 shows man-to-man pass coverage vs. a slot set to our right. The right end is the outside receiver to our left covered by the left half, and split end is the outside receiver to the right covered by the right half. The flanker back is the middle inside receiver covered by the safety. Since the tight cornerback is away from the flow, the split cornerback comes up to meet the flow. The offensive flankerback has no way of knowing he was not double covered until after the snap.

THE PREVENT DEFENSE

The 43 prevent defense is designed to stop the two minute offense. The defense is willing to sacrifice short gains since it has the clock on its side. It must not let their pass receivers get behind our defensive secondary for a touchdown. Naturally all prevent defenses will basically use zone pass coverages. Most two minute offenses use short side line pass patterns as a base, so they can get out of bounds and stop the clock. Basically we concentrate on an inside containment to prevent them from getting behind us, and discourage sideline and staircase patterns.

FIGURE 4-5 shows our 43 prevent defense against a pro set to our right. The sets, techniques, and responsibilities of each position are as follows:

TACKLES: Sets are to shade the outside shoulders of the offensive guards. They get control with a forearm shiver and they react laterally along the line of scrimmage without penetration.

ENDS: Both ends apply their basic outside pass rush. We only use a two man rush.

COMBO: Sets about two yards deeper than a middle linebacker would on a 53 call, and reacts to the side of the inside (middle) receiver.

TIGHT CORNERBACK AND MIDDLE LINEBACKER: Set on the outside shoulders of the two outside receivers, and apply the basic "bump and recovery" techniques. The only differences are they force the receivers to the inside on the bump, and after they have screened off the area between the passer and sidelines, they recover to the pre-snap triangle of the offensive

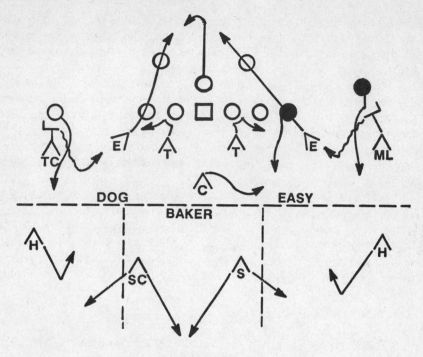

Figure 4-5
43 Prevent Defense

splits. This leaves our split side (backside) hook area open on a look in pattern, but we will give that to them.

HALFBACKS cover Able and Charlie respectively looking from the outside in. They must not let any receivers who enter their zones get behind them or to their outsides.

SAFETY AND SPLIT CORNERS: Both support their adjacent halfbacks to the inside and one another. They play the side of the inside receiver, or offensive backfield flow. The supporting backside back must not let any pass receiver get behind him in Baker.

We have found that the passer can get in trouble trying to dump it off to a backside receiver out of the backfield because of our "bump and recovery" technique.

PRIORITIES IN DEFENSIVE FUNDAMENTALS

Most tactical students are familiar with defensive approaches in basketball. A basketball player must first learn to play man-to-man defense before he can play zone defense. He cannot become fundamentally sound if he learns to play zone first, because he will become too independent on the team application to effectively carry out this individual assignment as he advances to a higher level of competition. These same principles apply with defensive secondary play in football, and they should first learn man-to-man coverage at the beginning levels. The reason coaches teach zone coverage at the lower levels is because it is easier to teach and apply as a team. This results in each individual player receiving poor defensive fundamentals.

Most basketball teams also have a basic defense built on sound fundamental techniques. They have a "press" in reserve that attacks the offense to force mistakes and turn overs. This results in the defense becoming an offense. Our stunting defensive system is applied in the same manner that a basketball team would apply a full court press.

We have completed the basic alignments, techniques, and responsibilities for our "combo" defensive system. We must perfect our basics before we add our stunts. Next is our combo stunting system for attacking and applying additional pressures on the offense.

5

STUNTING SYSTEM FOR THE "COMBO" DEFENSE

Our ends are the only two players who actually penetrate the line-of-scrimmage from our basic combo defense. The techniques of the rest of our defensive front are designed to fundamentally control the offense at the line of scrimmage. Our combo stunting system is designed to attack the offense with fast penetration. Since we are strictly a two platoon program, it offers our defensive players the same tactical challenges and incentives that we do our offensive players. Our players directly penetrate assigned gaps based on calls eliminating their basic control techniques they first applied on the offensive players. The players would love to call their own stunts on every play, but our coaching staff does not feel this would be fundamentally sound. The defensive coaches control the calls, and it keeps the players hungry with an appreciation for aggression. It prevents them from taking their basic responsibilities for granted. We only use stunts as we need them.

GAP CALLS FOR THE STUNTING SYSTEM

We number the gaps in their offensive line the same way we would number the holes in our own offensive line.

FIGURE 5-1 shows odd gaps (7 through 1) to the left, and even gaps (0 through 6) to the right. We attack and penetrate these gaps based on calls. 7, 5, 4, and 6 gaps are the calls applied by our exterior positions, and 3, 1, 0, and 2 gaps are the calls applied by our interior positions. Basically, our four linebackers and four down linemen work in teams of two, with two gaps assigned to each team. The linebacker shoots the gap that is called, and the down lineman shoots the remaining gap not called.

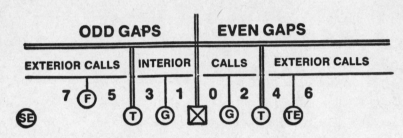

Figure 5-1
The Gap Call Stunt System

EXTERIOR GAP CALLS

The two ends, tight cornerback, and split cornerback apply the exterior gap calls. The left cornerback and end team up on 7 and 5 gap calls, and the right cornerback and end team up on 4 and 6 gap calls. Remember: The offensive split side and tight side alignments will determine to which side the cornerbacks flip-flop. Both cornerbacks shoot the gaps called and the two ends are responsible for the remaining gap not called.

FIGURE 5-2 shows the 5 or 4 gap calls for the exterior positions. The split cornerback is set to the left split side with the odd call, and the tight cornerback is set to the right tight side with the even call. The split cornerback shoots the 4 gap, and the tight cornerback shoots the 5 gap. Both ends use an old technique applied with the Oklahoma 54 defense. Both ends get outside shoulder control with a forearm shiver on the flanking offensive players, before their outside laterial pursuit with the line-of-scrimmage. The left end gets control on the slot back, and the right end gets control on the tight end.

FIGURE 5-3 shows the 7 or 6 gap calls for the exterior positions. The tight cornerback is set to the left tight side with the odd call, and the split

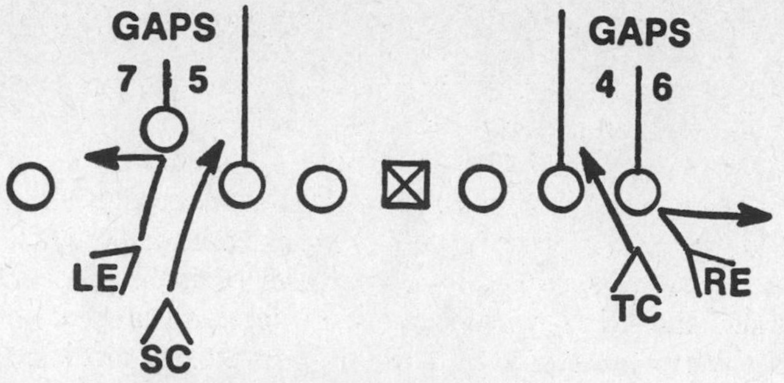

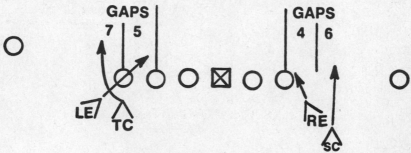

Figure 5-2
Exterior 5 and 4 Gap Calls

Figure 5-3
Exterior 7 and 6 Gap Calls

cornerback is set to the right split side with the even call. The left end shoots the 5 gap, and right end shoots the 4 gap. The tight cornerback shoots wide behind his left end, and the split corner back shoots wide behind his right end.

INTERIOR GAP CALLS

The two tackles, combo, and middle linebacker apply the interior gap calls. On a 44 defense the left tackle and combo team up on 3 and 1 gap calls, and the right tackle and middle linebacker team up on 0 and 2 gap calls. On a 53 defense the combo and middle linebacker team up on 1 and 0 gap calls. With interior stunt calls the interior defense ignore their basic set adjustments to the offensive split and tight side alignment. Regardless of the offensive line set, the whole interior defensive unit sets in a double stack alignment on 44 calls, and a balanced combo middle linebacker stack alignment on 53 calls.

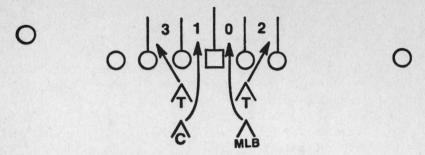

Figure 5-4
Interior 1 and 0 Gap Calls (44 Defense)

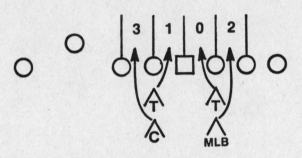

Figure 5-5
Interior 3 and 2 Gap Calls (44 Defense)

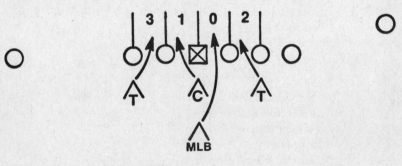

Figure 5-6
Interior 0 Gap Call (53 Defense)

FIGURE 5-4 shows the 1 or 0 gap 44 calls for the interior positions. The combo shoots the 1 gap, and the middle linebacker shoots the 0 gap. The left tackle shoots the 3 gap, and the right tackle shoots the 2 gap.

FIGURE 5-5 shows the 3 or 2 gap 44 calls for the interior positions. The combo shoots the 3 gap, and middle linebacker shoots the 2 gap. The left tackle shoots the 1 gap, and the right tackle shoots the 0 gap.

FIGURE 5-6 shows the 0 gap, 53 call for the interior positions. The left and right tackles set on their offensive tackles, and shoot their respective 3 and 2 gaps. The combo shoots the 1 gap, and the middle linebacker shoots the 0 gap.

FIGURE 5-7 shows the 1 gap, 53 call for the interior positions. The left and right tackles again set on their offensive tackles, and shoot their respective 3 and 2 gaps. The combo shoots the 0 gap and the middle linebacker shoots the 1 gap. (Figure 5-8)

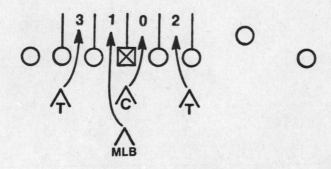

Figure 5-7
Interior 1 Gap Call (53 Defense)

All of these gap calls can be made by each two man team independent of one another. They can be applied along with our basic combo defense in any area where the offense might have found a weak spot.

THE SAFETY BLITZ

The safety blitz is a stunt that was developed in the pro-ranks. We feel it can even be more effective at the high school level in a passing situation, such as third down and long yardage. We get a heavy pass rush to sack a quarterback, while maintaining man-to-man pass coverage. 44 safety blitz is a team call. We first make our defensive set adjustments to their offensive tight and split side alignments. The safety makes his gap call after his tight side adjustment. The defensive tackle to the tight side sets on his offensive tackle and

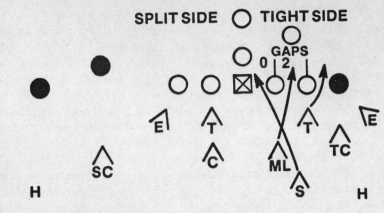

8A - 0 or 2 Gap Calls

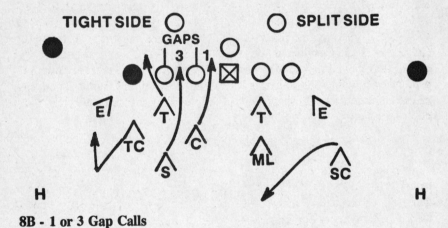

8B - 1 or 3 Gap Calls

Figure 5-8
Safety Blitz

shoots his outside gap. Either the combo or middle linebacker shoots his respective interior gap that is not called. The safety shoots the gap that he calls. The defensive front to the split side applies their basic 44 stack assignments.

FIGURE 5-8 shows the differences in a 44 safety blitz as a result of adjusting to offensive variations:

Figure 5-8A shows a 44 safety blitz against a slot set to our left. This gives us a split side to our left and a tight side to our right. We use man-to-man coverage. Our left half covers the split end, and our right half covers the tight end who are the two outside receivers. The split cornerback covers the slot back who is the inside (middle) receiver. The left end, left tackle and combo apply their basic 44 stack assignments to the left split side. The right defensive front and safety set in a split 44 alignment to the offensive tight side for an even gap call. The right end and tight cornerback apply their basic assignments. The right tackle shoots the outside gap. The safety makes a 0 gap call, and shoots the 0 gap behind the middle linebacker who shoots the 2 gap. If he had made a 2 gap call, the middle linebacker would have shot the 0 gap.

Figure 5-8B shows a 44 safety blitz against a pro-set to our right. This gives us a tight side to our left, and a split side to our right. Again we apply man-to-man coverage. Our left half covers the flanker back, and our right half covers the split end who are the two outside receivers. Our tight cornerback must cover the tight end who is the inside (middle) receiver. This means he will not apply his normal "bump and recover" technique. The right end, right tackle, middle linebacker, and split cornerback apply their basic 44 stack assignments to the right split side. The left defensive front and safety set in a split 44 alignment to the offensive tight side for an odd gap call. The left tackle shoots the outside gap. The safety makes a 3 gap call, and the combo shoots the 1 gap. If he had made 1 gap call, the combo would have shot the 3 gap. After studying our 44 safety blitz, I'm sure you will find it sound, and can see how it can really shake-up a high school quarterback, even when you don't sack him.

GOAL LINE DEFENSES

Our goal line and short yardage defenses are an outgrowth of stunting techniques. There are two kinds of short yardage situation, and we have a defense for each one. There are situations where the offense needs a yard or more, and might try for more with a pass. Here we use our 83 goal line defense. There are other situations where the offense need only inches, and neither side will be concerned with a pass. Here we use our 65 goal line defense.

FIGURE 5-9 shows an 83 goal line defense applied against a floater T backfield set. It is a situation where the offense needs a couple of yards and might pass. The two ends, two tackles, combo, and middle linebacker shoot their respective gaps. Both the tight and split cornerbacks apply a "bump and outside" technique. They pick up any back coming out of the backfield man-to-man. Both halfbacks key the outside receivers, and the safety keys the inside (middle) receiver. If their keys try to block they come up fast to the outside of the keys. They are responsible for man-to-man pass coverage.

FIGURE 5-10 shows a 65 goal line defense applied against a full house tight T formation. It is a situation where the offense only need inches, and we

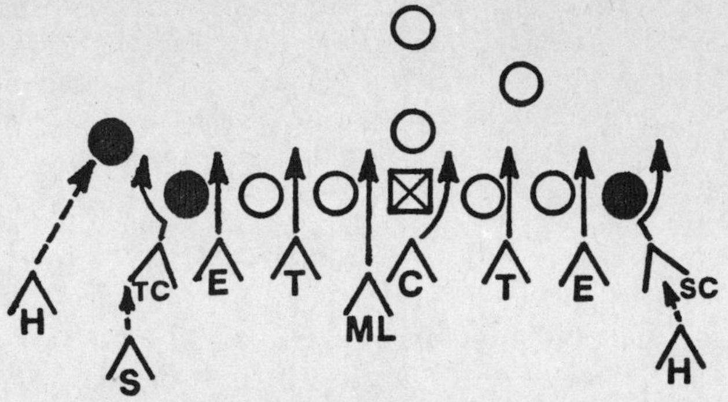

Figure 5-9
83 Goal Line Defense

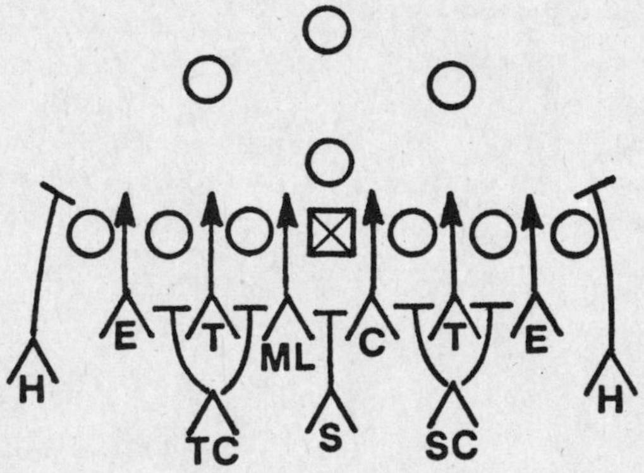

Figure 5-10
65 Goal Line Defense

both know they will go for it. A common practice is for the back to dive over the line after he takes a hand-off, or a power play from an "I" tailback set. The two ends, two tackles, combo, and middle linebacker shoot their respective gaps as they did on an 83 call. The halfbacks, cornerbacks and safety fill high. The six down linemen fill the holes and stop the ball carrier, while the five backers hit the ball carrier high to prevent his momentum from carrying him forward and picking up those needed inches.

We have all seen times where successful goal line efforts were the highlight and turning point of the game. There is nothing as demoralizing as for an offense to march the length of the field only to be stopped for four downs on the goal line. This usually shifts the momentum to the defensive team. Even though the defensive team's back has been left against the wall their offensive unit very often can break them out of the hole, while the opposition is still in a mental state of limbo.

6

RELATING THE DRILLS TO THE "COMBO" TECHNIQUES

Time is the biggest factor in teaching the techniques for the basic combo defense. Techniques are learned skills, and must be continuously practiced in order to perfect them to the point that they become second nature in reaction. This must be accomplished without becoming bored with mental staleness because of repetition. Skills must be learned through related drills in a limited amount of practice time.

If every coach and player does not know exactly what they are going to be doing in a given block of practice time, their anticipations of "Whats next?" can make practice a drag, and lead to doubts as to reasons and purposes. Any time players are standing around with their hands in their britches, it is a sure sign of disorganization and doubts. We use a black board with time blocks for our practice schedule that is divided into individual, unit, and team workouts. Each coach fills in what he needs to cover for the following day, immediately after practice. Afterwards, the head coach blocks in the times. It is displayed for the players before practice. They study it without being told, and know exactly what to expect, and what they will be doing. Our average practice schedules are exactly one hour and fifty minutes: No more or no less. Occasionally, as a head coach, I would forget, and we would extend a few minutes. Every time I did, it seemed to result in a freak, key injury. My Chief Assistant would comment "One thing's for sure; we'll finish at 5:30 sharp for the rest of this year." My reply was simply, "You had better believe it."

Only use drills that are related to individual techniques and team application. There must be a carry-over learning situation from the drills to actual applications. It sometimes amazes me how a few drill happy coaches can use drills that have no carry over value, when they are not close to being related to the players' application. A coach is a teacher, and the learning situations must have carry over values. I have learned to excuse a few teachers who become so academic minded, they lose perspective as to their purpose. This does not excuse a coach for not relating between his means and ends. Remember: they don't keep score in a class room, but they sure do on the field. As an example: why teach a defensive down lineman a tip drill, or why teach a defensive safety a four point stance. As ridiculous as this may seem, I have seen this done at a few higher levels than mine. Relate your drills to the techniques that your players will be using in realistic application.

There are two types of drills with carryover values that we apply to each position. They are individual and unit drills. We then follow up with team application. This is our basis for a practice schedule.

INDIVIDUAL DRILLS

Individual drills are learned skills that must carry over to a team function. Our ends, tackles, combos, and middle linebackers use the same set of individual drills. Sometimes we include the tight cornerback. Our halfbacks, safeties and cornerbacks use a different set of individual drills. We apply these drills as our second phase of warm ups following calisthenics. This includes both pre-practice and pre-game warmups.

Keep in mind that the defense reacts on sight and movement and not sound. Try and start all drills from the movement of the football, and try to end them in a controlled hitting position.

The following set of individual drills are related to the techniques that are used by the defensive front.

FIGURE 6-1: The purpose of the SNAP drill is to teach the defensive front to get off with the snap of the ball, or the movement of an offensive player. The coach uses a lot of pre-snap signals testing the defensive non-reactions to sound. As elementary as this may seem, it is often neglected and not realized, until the offense draws the defense off side with extended snap signals. The best coaching point is to tell defensive players to turn off their hearing aids and use their eye balls, after they have jumped off sides. They

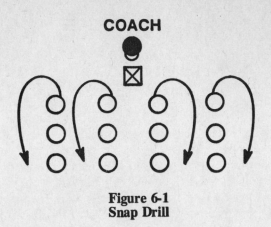

Figure 6-1
Snap Drill

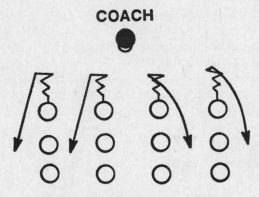

Figure 6-2
Agility and Reaction Drill

will get the point. Sound should not distract defensive players.

FIGURE 6-2: The purposes of *AGILITY drills* are to teach the defensive front to react to movement based on sight, and at the same time maintain body control for hitting positions. Our hitting position is done with short choppy steps for balance, and in a low crouched position with the head up. When the coach raises the ball, is the signal to begin a hitting position, and when he lowers it is the signal to drop to all fours. He can motion the players forward, backward, left or right while they are in either an all fours or hitting position. All responsies are to the motion of the ball.

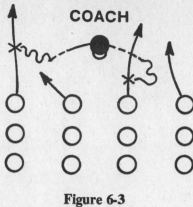

Figure 6-3
Scoop Drill

FIGURE 6-3: The purpose of the *SCOOP drill* is simply to teach the defensive front how to pick up a loose ball and run for the goal. Fumbles happen in the course of a season more than we realize, and too often defensive linemen do not know how to react to this surprising situation. They know what the results can be, and it's their one shot opportunity to score a touchdown. The coaching points are to not get excited and over run the ball. With body control scoop the ball from behind with one hand into the other extended forehand. If you don't have immediate control of the ball, fall on it. You will lose it on a second attempt. Can you remember a season where you never saw a big defensive lineman pick up a fumble and run half the field for a touchdown? How many times have you seen them keep knocking it all over the field like a greased pig? Those opportunities present themselves often enough so that a few minutes of scoop drill in each practice is worthwhile. The coach keeps two balls going in a scoop drill. One is for the two lines on his right, and the other is for the two lines on his left. This keeps the drill running fast and smooth.

FIGURE 6-4 The purposes of the *SHIVER drill* are to teach hitting position, reaction, defensive control, and recovery to our defensive front. The offensive line is finished with their drills on the seven man sled by the time the defensive front finishes their first three or four drills. This leaves the 7 man sled vacated for the shiver drill. Each player takes a hitting position, delivers a forearm shiver, gets inside control, and then recovers seven times from left to right. When everyone has completed the drill they repeat it from right to left.

FIGURE 6-5 The purpose of our *TACKLING drill* is to teach the correct

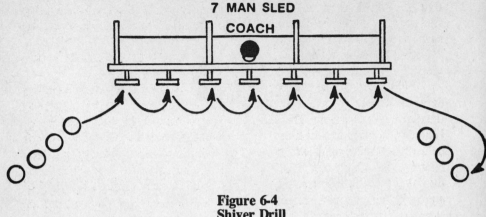

Figure 6-4
Shiver Drill

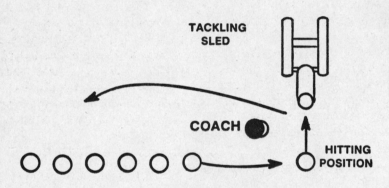

Figure 6-5
Tackling Drill

techniques after contact. Many may not be familiar with a tackling sled, but it has the same values to the defense that a blaster or 7 man sled has to the offense. It is simply a single, light weight tackling dummy mounted on two balanced, heavy weight pontoons. If you don't make good contact, and maintain aggressive body control with balanced leg drive; it will whip you. It bounces right back up after being knocked over. We had an all conference offensive guard lose a bit of pride with a defensive player, because he couldn't block it. He kept losing contact and control with his leg drive in his follow through. He will not refer to it as a one man blocking sled again. The tackling sled is the basis for the drill. Later in the season it is also used following the snap, agility, and shiver drills.

The following set of individual drills are related to the techniques that are used by the defensive secondary:

FIGURE 6-6 The purpose of the *ONE-ON-ONE drill* is to teach the defensive secondary man-to-man coverage. The receiver tries to get as close to the defender as possible. The defender back pedals until he feels the receiver is getting in range to beat him. We do not like the back pedal, and we do not believe in turning our heads on the ball. We simply keep a facing shoulder relationship with the ball, the receiver, and the sideline. The key to this is for the defender to be able to change directions with the receiver, and maintaining a proper facing shoulder relation with the passer by using a quick cross over step. Our one-on-one drill is designed to pass to the receiver at three points. First is the inside hook, and the defender has a left shoulder relationship, with the sideline to the right. Second, the receiver breaks to the sideline and the defender still has a left shoulder relationship after his cross-over step. The sideline is now the defenders best friend, and the only thing the receiver has left to do is to cut up field on a staircase pattern. Third the defender must pivot on a crossover step, and run full speed up the field with a right shoulder relationship to the ball. If a defender can learn to do this he can play man-to-man coverage. If he can play man-to-man defense he will have no trouble with deep zone coverage. This is our basic defensive secondary drill, and we use it on the left sideline as much as we do on the right.

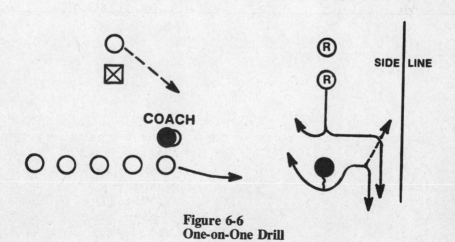

Figure 6-6
One-on-One Drill

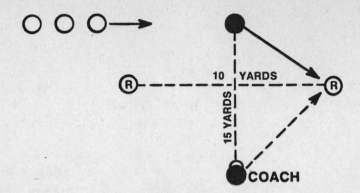

Figure 6-7
Break Drill

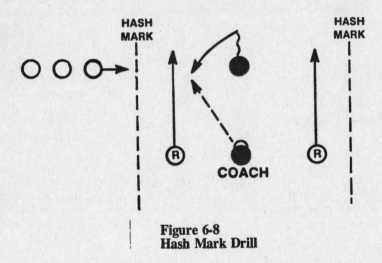

Figure 6-8
Hash Mark Drill

FIGURE 6-7 The purposes of the *BREAK drill* are to teach the pass defender how to get the jump on the ball, and to judge the distance of the ball while it is in the air. We have two stationary receivers set 10 yards apart. They are bisected by a receiver (5 yards), and a coach (10 yards) who are set 15 yards apart. The receiver always breaks at the time, and in the direction that the coach steps. The object is for the receiver to intercept the ball by cutting it off on his break before it reaches the receiver.

FIGURE 6-8 The purpose of the *HASH MARK drill* is to teach pass defenders that they can cover two receivers in a deep zone by maintaining a good position and breaking with the ball. The two receivers must stay inside the hash marks. After the defender has gained confidence in his ability to cover both receivers, the coach can test his anticipation. This is done by the coach increasing the distance of his set, faking to one receiver, and then throwing to another.

FIGURE 6-9 The purposes of the *WAVE drill* are to teach reaction to the ball, body control, and to quickly change directions with a crossover step.

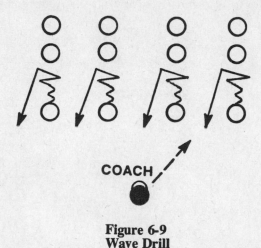

Figure 6-9
Wave Drill

FIGURE 6-10 The purpose of the *TIP drill* is to teach pass defenders to react to the ball when it is thrown to a receiver in front of them. We start out with two defenders from a single file. The first defender tips the ball and the second defender intercepts. As we progress into the season we use the multiple tip drill as illustrated in Figure 6-10. This teaches reaction when the ball is thrown to the opposite side of the field. With our basic four deep secondary it is tip, tip, tip, and then an interception.

FIGURE 6-11 The purpose of the *COMEBACK drill* is to teach the pass defender to come back for the ball from some distance. He must return at a fast low position reading the arms of the receiver. He maintains an outside foot before a forward roll on the interception.

FIGURE 6-12 The purpose of the *MIRROR drill* is to build the defender's confidence that he can maintain body control, and a hitting position in the open field. The defender meets the ball carrier in the open field at controlled speed. After he is in range he maintains his hitting position with short choppy

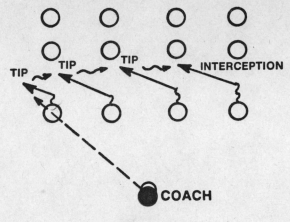

Figure 6-10
Tip Drill

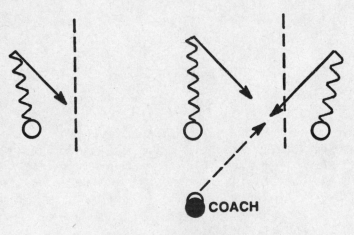

Figure 6-11
Comeback Drill

steps while the ball carrier tries to make any type of motion while in a stationary position, and the defender must match it. The ball carrier can break upon a signal from the coach. Either the defender has or has not lost position and control. The players love this drill, and it always results in something funny happening. We use our offensive split ends without the ball. It has as

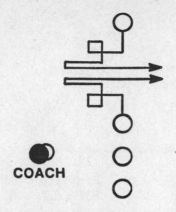

Figure 6-12
Mirror Drill

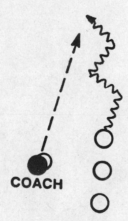

Figure 6-13
Weave Drill

much carry over value for our split ends in their blocking techniques, as it does for our defenders.

FIGURE 6-13 The purposes of our *WEAVE drill* are to teach the cross over step to change directions, and to keep a proper shoulder relationship with the ball. The drill ends when the coach throws the ball to the defender.

This completes the individual drills for both our defensive front and secondary. This may seem like a lot of drills in each set, but as the season progresses the units should be able to complete them in 10 to 15 minutes. Change-up the sequence, add competitive motivations, and integrate the relationships to their function to prevent them from becoming a bore.

UNIT DRILLS

Our opening unit drills only involve the defensive units. Our remaining-ing unit drills involve both the offensive and defensive units with related competitive responsibilities.

The following unit drills involve our defensive interior front, plus the tight cornerbacks. Because our defensive ends' techniques and responsibilities are so different, they must use another drill during this time.

FIGURE 6-14 The purposes of the interior unit drills are to teach interior set adjustments, forearm shivers, control, and reaction to responsibilities on the 7 man sled. The tight cornerbacks learn their "bump and recovery" techniques. The three passers throw to the reaction of middle linebacker, and the recovery of the cornerbacks.

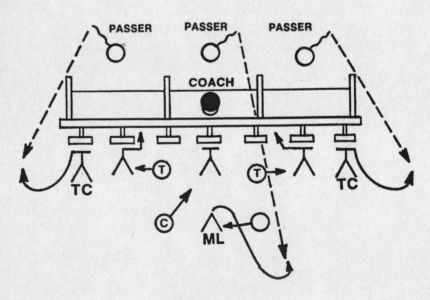

Figure 6-14
Interior Unit Drill

FIGURE 6-15 The purpose of the defensive end drill is to teach them proper reaction to the quarterback's movement. The tires simulate the offensive tackles and tight ends. As soon as the ball is snapped the defensive end's first responsibilities are to get to spots two yards behind the offensive tackles with inside shoulder relationships to the quarterback. From that point on they react to the quarterback's movement while maintaining the same inside shoulder relationship. This drill can also be applied against a skeleton offensive backfield to teach both the offense and the defense responses and reactions to the options.

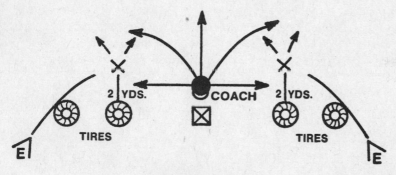

Figure 6-15
Defensive End Drill

After these two unit drills have been completed, the defensive ends joint the interior units, and the tight cornerbacks join the defensive secondary units for their following respective unit drills against skeleton offensive units.

FIGURE 6-16 The purposes of the UNIT TIME drill are to teach the defensive front the pass rush, and the offensive line pass blocking. The offensive coach uses a stop-watch. It is a very live and competitive drill controlled by the offensive and defensive line coaches. If the offense can keep the defense from tagging the passer for four seconds they win. If the defense can tag the passer within three seconds they win. Anything between three and four seconds, it is a draw. The passer ends the drill by throwing to stationary receivers in the hook zone after a four second whistle. This is to test the reactions of the combo and middle linebacker. Both offensive and defensive line coaches make the necessary coaching points between times.

FIGURE 6-17 The purposes of the unit pass drill are to teach the defensive secondary (half backs, safeties, and tight and split cornerbacks) pass defense, and the offensive backs and ends pass offense. Both the offensive and defensive backfield coaches are in position to make coaching points.

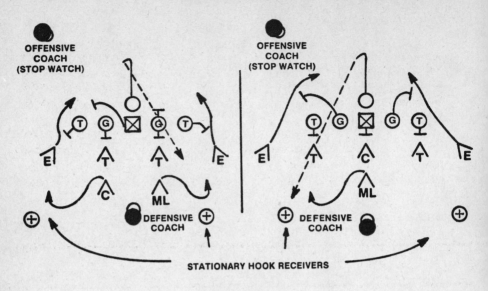

Figure 6-16
Unit Time Drill

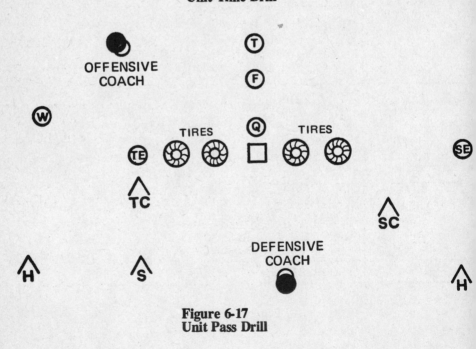

Figure 6-17
Unit Pass Drill

TEAM APPLICATION

As was earlier stated, our practice schedules are based on related individual and unit drills followed by team application. As we progress into the season we reduce and alternate the time blocks for our individual and unit drills, and work in our next opponent's defensive and offensive teams based on scouting reports.

FIGURE 6-18 Shows an example of our typical pre-season practice schedule. It is self explanatory. Our individual drills are set in a 20 minute time block, and our unit drills are set in a 30 minute time block. Team application is set in a 45 minute time block. As we progress into the season all

HUSKIES' PRACTICE SCHEDULE	YES PADS 5 SEPT X3			
TIMES COACHES	OFFENSE REAVES BORDERS		DEFENSE LAVENDER GREEN	
3:30	15 MINS. TEAM CALISTHENICS			
3:45 INDIV. DRILLS	BACKS & S.E. BLASTER OPTION	LINES & T.E.s *AGILITIES *7 MAN SLED *REVIEW PASS BLOCKING	FRONT SNAP REACTION SHIVER TACKLING	SECONDARY WAVE TIP COMEBACK MIRROR HASH MARK ONE-ON-ONE
4:05	5 MIN. ICE BREAK			
4:10 UNIT DRILLS	PASS OFF VS. TIME VS. PASS RUSH		PASS DEF	
TEAM APPLICATION 4:35 5:00 5:15	VARSITY VS. VARSITY – J.VS VS. J.V.S. (CONTROL-REACTION) 30-40-70-80 POWER SERIES – BASIC 44 and 53 DEF. QUICK DRAW OFFENSE – 43 PREVENT DEF. PLAY THE GAME – FULL SCRIMMAGE G GOAL LINE OFF – SHORT YARDAGE DEF.			
5:25	PROGRESSIVE SPRINTS			

Figure 6-18
Practice Schedule

drills are reduced into a 30 minute time block, and our total team application is increased to one hour and fifteen minutes.

Now that we have completed all of the basic elements and principles for the "combo" defensive system we have the tactical ingredients to put them into team application. The tactical ingredients alone are strictly academic. We need to add opponent's tactical and personnel offensive tendencies based on current films and scouting reports. This require a lot of time and effort with limitations in short-cuts. Next we will give our method of adjusting the "combo" defensive system to offensive tendencies.

7

ADJUSTING THE COMBO SYSTEM TO OFFENSIVE TENDENCIES

Both our defensive and offensive game plans are based on scouting reports, statistics, tactical team characteristics, and personnel tendencies. Since the defenses must adjust to offense, it usually takes a lot more time and effort to formulate a defensive game plan, than it does for the offense. It must begin with the scouting reports which are made up of both tactical and personnel charts. The tactical charts are plotted for tendencies and then related to the reports on their individual offensive personnel. This relationship is finally formulated into a defensive game plan within the framework of adjusting it to our combo system. This usually has to be done by our defensive coaches during the two day weekend, outside of current game responsibilities. Saturday nights and Sundays are very busy times for our coaching staff during the regular season. We know of one team in our league who used a computer in charting tendencies, but have very little idea of how effective their system was. With our resources, we had to manually chart, and interpret tendencies. The following process is the method that we used.

SCOUTING REPORTS

A review of past films, scouting reports, and tactical systems are preliminary preparations needed in scouting an opponent. The more familiar you are with them, the easier they will be to scout. It usually takes two coaches working together to get an accurate report.

FIGURE 7-1 shows a sample of our basic scouting forms with panels for charting each play. This particular offensive team that we used for an example ran 51 total plays during the game, and our scouts used five pages of this form to chart their offense. Pass plays are charted on another form. There are places to chart field position, hash mark, down, yardage, gain, formation, backfield action, blocking, and series in a very rapid order of thinking. The series is the number of plays during a single possession or offensive control of the ball. The number of the play within a series is shown in the lower left corner, and is used to plot tendencies. The formation is charted by circling the +'s in the diagram. Anyone that has scouted knows that you are so busy charting, and using time out's, halftime, or after the game filling in anything you missed, that you don't know what you have. It is only later when you begin to plot and break it down, that what you have charted begins to come into focus.

STATISTICS

Defensive statistics are the test and measurements in the evaluation of what our individuals or team have done, and can only have a motivating influence on what we are going to do. We apply tackling charts, and recognize individual efforts using similiar methods as most teams do. This is only self-evaluation for a team, and does not evaluate our opponents. We cannot keep statistics on our opponents as we do ourselves. It is important that we recognize the difference between statistics, and plotting offensive tendencies. It would be impossible to evaluate an opponent as well as we do ourselves. I have never been sure what is meant by the quote, "Statistics are for losers." I have observed that winners apply more statistics than losers, but they keep them in proper perspective without using them as a crutch. The score board must have priority over statistics, and the means of preparation is more important than statistics. We all have statistics, but we all can't win. Plotting tendencies are based on the future, and statistics are based on the past. There is a difference!

PLOTTING TACTICAL TENDENCIES

We plot their tactical tendencies from our scouting reports. If we have

BASIC SCOUTING FORM – DATE 22 SEPT. X3 OPP. CENTRAL

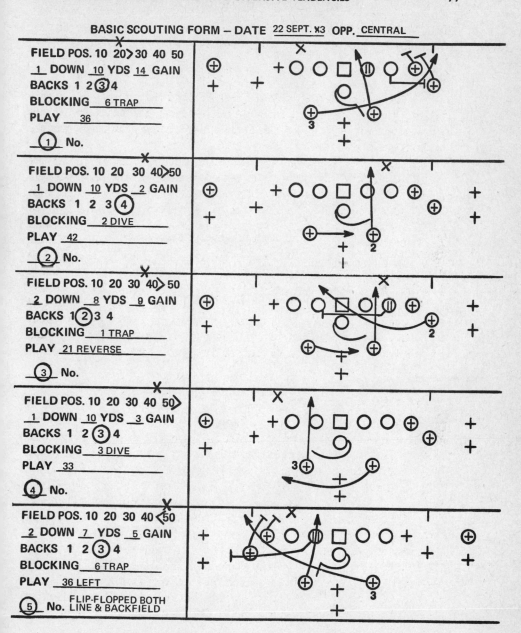

FIELD POS. 10 20>30 40 50
_1_ DOWN _10_ YDS _14_ GAIN
BACKS 1 2 ③ 4
BLOCKING___6 TRAP___
PLAY ___36___
① No.

FIELD POS. 10 20 30 40>50
_1_ DOWN _10_ YDS _2_ GAIN
BACKS 1 2 3 ④
BLOCKING___2 DIVE___
PLAY _42_
② No.

FIELD POS. 10 20 30 40> 50
_2_ DOWN _8_ YDS _9_ GAIN
BACKS 1 ② 3 4
BLOCKING___1 TRAP___
PLAY _21 REVERSE_
③ No.

FIELD POS. 10 20 30 40 50>
_1_ DOWN _10_ YDS _3_ GAIN
BACKS 1 2 ③ 4
BLOCKING___3 DIVE___
PLAY _33_
④ No.

FIELD POS. 10 20 30 40 <50
_2_ DOWN _7_ YDS _5_ GAIN
BACKS 1 2 ③ 4
BLOCKING___6 TRAP___
PLAY _36 LEFT_
⑤ No. FLIP-FLOPPED BOTH
LINE & BACKFIELD

Figure 7-1
Scouting Reports for Defense

PLOTTING OFFENSIVE TACTICAL TENDENCIES CENTRAL 22 SEPT X3

PLOT FROM BASIC SCOUTING FORM.				(ODD) HOLES (EVEN)										(ODD) HOLES (EVEN)									
NO	DN	YD	GN	9	7	5	3	1	0	2	4	6	8	9	7	5	3	1	0	2	4	6	8
1	1	10	14							+14													
2	1	10	2							+2													
3	2	8	9				+9																
4	1	10	3				+3																
5	2	7	3												+5								
6	3	2	3								+3												
7	1	10	3							+3													
8	2	7	3									+3											
9	3	4	2							+2													
10	PUNT		23	PUNT																			
1	1	10	3							+3													
2	2	7	2			+2						+7	FUMBLE – DEFENSE RECOVERS										
1	1	10	1					+1															
2	2	9	2							+2													
3	3	7	12	PASS COMPLETE (WB IN DOG) THEIR PLAY ACTION – OUR 6 PATTERN																			
4	1	10	3							3													
5	2	7	42	TOUCHDOWN +42 EP. GOOD																			
1	1	10	2													+2							
2	2	8	3												+3								
3	3	5	1															1					
4	4	4	36	PUNT																			
1	1	10	4							+4													
2	2	6	1				1																
3	3	5	36	TOUCHDOWN PASS (TE IN DOG) FAKED INSIDE REVERSE																			

22	PLAYS
2	PASSES
2	PUNTS
2	T.D.s
1	FUMBLE
64	TOTAL PLAYS

SPLIT — OPTION — BACKSIDE — FRONT SIDE   FRONT SIDE — OPTION — SPLIT — BACKSIDE

| MOST OF FIRST HALF SHORT OF ONE SERIES 4 PLAYS | THIS IS THEIR BASIC FORMATION SET TO THE RIGHT WITH THEIR BASIC FRONTSIDE-BACKSIDE BACK-FIELD PATTERNS. THEY HAVE A RIGHT HANDED TENDENCY RUNNING 2/3's OF THEIR PLAYS TO RIGHT. | THEY FLIP-FLOP THEIR WHOLE TEAM TO GO FORMATION TO THE ELFT. THEY WERE ONLY IN THIS SET FOR ONE SERIES AND FOUR PLAYS. |

Figure 7-2
Plotting for Defensive Game Plan

two current scouting reports against common opponents with different defensive characteristics, then we feel we can get a good evaluation of them.

FIGURE 7-2 shows how the plotting of our scouting report forms patterns that repeat themselves. All offensive systems have one, two, or three basic backfield patterns or series. They use certain plays and point-of-attack based on downs, yardage, and field position. We have found that we can basically plot most offensive systems within the framework of this plotting form, regardless of how multiple and complex they might seem. They can change their formations and sets, but they cannot change their techniques and basic patterns within their system. This particular offensive system is a winged T with a split backfield. The basic set has a strongside to their right, and a weakside to their left. They run a dive, second man through, and inside reverse sequence to the strongside, and the option series to the weakside. They will flip-flop the whole backfield and line to get the set strong to their left. This is to utilize the strengths and weaknesses of their personnel, but also leaves outstanding strongside and weakside tendencies. Notice that the first five plots are taken from the first page of our scouting report. This game was plotted within two pages. Special plays and passes are diagramed on cue cards to be used by our offensive scouting team in practice.

EVALUATING OFFENSIVE PERSONNEL

The evaluation of their personnel is the second phase of a scouting report. Tactics are strictly academic without personnel. It is individual personalities that make up the characteristics of a team, and determine tactical tendencies. Good coaches adjust their tactical tendencies to fit their individual types of players that they are working with at the present time, and then try to conceal them from the outside. Evaluation of personnel is usually based on outside observations, studies, and judgements.

FIGURE 7-3 shows the scouting form used to chart their personnel. The best evaluation is by two scouts working independently of one another on separate occasions. Afterwards you can compare reports, and where they are different requires a third opinion. The basis for evaluating personnel usually begins with the eligibility roster and a game program.

Match and compare the evaluation of their personnel with the plotted tactical tendencies. You will surely find some related patterns between the two forms from which to establish a game plan.

THE DEFENSIVE GAME PLAN

Most of the time when the offense scores on the defense, it was not the results of being caught by surprise. The defense knew what they did, and how they got beat. It was not something that they had not been told and shown in

OFFENSIVE PERSONNEL FORM____CENTRAL – 22 SEPT X3____

POSITION	NO.	NAME	WT.	HT.	EVALUATION
BACKFIELD	41	STEVE TODD	165	5'10"	BACKS UP 43 – NOT AS EFFECITVE
QUARTERBACKS	12	DON MURRAY	180	6'1"	GOOD MECHANICS – ACCURATE ON SHORT PASS. WANTS TO KEEP THE BALL ON BACKSIDE OPTION (ANTICI-PATES) STRONG BALL CARRIER – QUICK
WINGBACK	27	BILL ROLWES	160	5'9"	VERY FAST – WEAK BLOCKER – WILL BURN YOU ON REVERSE AND SHORT RECEPTIONS.
FULLBACK	31	DON SMITH	195	5'11'	HARD RUNNER, GOOD BLOCKER
TAILBACK	43	H. MANNS	170	6'1"	BEST BACK – CARRIES 1/3 OF TIME. DANGEROUS IN OPEN FIELD. FAST – LIKES TO TURN BACK AGAINST GRAIN.
CENTERS	54	FRANK MATHEWS	205	6'2"	GOOD SNAP – SCREEN BLOCKER – GOOD PASS BLOCKER – NOSE MAN SEEMS TO BOTHER HIM.
ENDS SE	81	GARRY PITTS	165	5'10"	GOOD HAND – NOT A LOT OF SPEED – WILL NOT NEED DOUBLE COVERAGE AS LAST WEEK
TE	83	BOB RAKER	205	6'2"	GOOD BLOCKER, EXCELLENT HANDS PASS TO HIM IN TIGHT SPOT
TE	87	JOE SANDERS	175	5'11'	GOOD BLOCKER – REPLACES 81 AS DOUBLE TE
TACKLES STRONGSIDE	77	DAN BIRCHFIELD	210	6'3"	STRONG BLOCKER EXCELLENT TRAPPER ON REVERSE
BACKSIDE	65	BOB MATECKI	205	6'1"	BIG AND STRONG – BUT DOESN'T SEEM TO USE IT. NOT AGGRESSIVE – DON'T WAKE HIM UP.
GUARDS STRONGSIDE	61	KEN BENZ	190	5'11"	BEST OFFENSIVE BLOCKER – BOTH STRAIGHT AHEAD AS A PULLER, AHEAD AS A PULLER, ALL CONFERENCE
BACKSIDE	63	B. COSGROVE	195	6'	FAIR BLOCKER STRAIGHT AHEAD. WILL PASS UP OUR INSIDE L.B. s WHEN PULLING THROUGH HOLES.

Figure 7-3
Personnel Tendencies for Defensive Game Plan

practice. The defense probably did not know exactly WHEN to expect a certain successful offensive play. We try to use their offensive tendencies to project WHEN they will apply certain tactics, or use certain personnel in the formulation of our defensive game plans. Anyone who can do this on every play will stop every play.

FIGURE 7-4 shows our defensive game plan based on their tactical and personnel tendencies. The first part is the diagnostic results. There is one very interesting tactical tendency that we will try and exploit. 65 to 70% of the ball exchanges in their backfield patterns take place behind the gap of their offensive tackle and guard to our left. Their offensive tackle takes a maximum split. We will penetrate that area with stunts or blitzes to pressure their timing, and mess things up.

The second part is their offensive sets and personnel, and the third part is our defensive adjustments and calls.

On 44 calls we will apply our basic adjustments to both their basic set right and flip-flop to their left. We will use a 44 call on second or third downs, with seven or more yards to go. The defensive secondary will use zone coverage. We will use 3 gap calls on stunts and blitzes to their basic set on our left, and 2 gap calls on stunts and blitzes to their flip-flop set on our right.

We will use our basic 53 calls and adjustments on first down and short yardage situation. The defensive secondary will use man-to-man coverage. We will use a 1 gap call on a stunt to their basic set on our left, and a 0 gap call on a stunt to their flip-flop set on our right.

The defensive game plan must be completed before Monday morning preceding the game. Their personnel evaluation and defensive game plan both must be graphically reproduced to put into the hands of the players. Most of Monday's practice time is spent in the squad room studying films and having chalk talks. The first phase is to review the films of the game we have just completed, and the statistics that are related to it. The second phase is to introduce the tactical and personnel tendencies of our next opponent. After we have presented our game plan, we will look at any films we have on them. If it is a Friday game we will finish with a very short workout. If it is a Saturday game, we won't even dress out.

Our individual and unit drills are reduced to twenty-five minutes in our practice schedule, and our team application is increased to one hour and twenty minutes. Forty minutes of that team application are workouts against scouting teams using cue cards.

The remainder of this book will be devoted to the tactical adjustments of the combo defense against every type of offense that you might have to play against. There becomes a large variation in our defense adjustments against the different problems that different defenses present. A few outsider have accused us of having a multiple defense, but actually we are making adjustments to a variation in offenses from one week to the next.

DEFENSIVE GAME PLAN _____ CENTRAL — HOME 19X3 _____

I. DIAGNOSTIC RESULTS OF OFFENSIVE TACTICAL & PERSONNEL TENDENCIES

1. GOT OFF 51 OFFENSIVE PLAYS — SCORED 20 PTS.
2. 47 PLAYS WERE RUN OUT OF THEIR SET TO OUR LEFT.
   FLIP-FLOPPED 4 TIMES TO OUR RIGHT.
3. THEY HAVE A RIGHT-HAND TENDENCY SINCE 2/3's (34) OF THEIR PLAYS WERE RUN TO OUR LEFT, AND THEIR BEST OFFENSIVE LINEMEN ARE SET TO THE STRONGSIDE OF THEIR SET.
4. 36 IS THEIR FAVORITE PLAY IN A SHORT YARDAGE SITUATION, AND THEY LIKE THEIR INSIDE REVERSE ON 1ST OR 2 DOWN WITH 6 OR MORE YARDS TO GO.
5. ARE CONSERVATIVE. HIT 3 OF 5 PASSES.
6. MAX SPLITS BETWEEN TACKLE & GUARD TO THEIR STRONG-SIDE. OVER 70% OF BACKFIELD ACTION TAKES PLACE 2 YARDS BEHIND THAT GAP. WE WILL STUNT IT.

Figure 7-4
Defensive Game Plan

II. BASIC OFFENSIVE FORMATION (LEFT FLIP-FLOPS TO RIGHT)

PLAYED 13 PLAYERS — WE WILL TACTICALLY ADJUST TO THEIR RIGHT & LEFT SETS WITHOUT FLIP-FLOPPING OUR INTERIOR FRONT.	
DEFENSIVE ADJUSTMT.	
<u>44 CALL</u> — BASIC SET ADJUSTMENTS TO FLIP-FLOP <u>STUNTS</u> — 3 GAP CALL <u>BLITZ</u> — 3 GAP CALL PASSING DOWN & YARDAGE	
<u>53 CALL</u> — BASIC SET ADJUSTMENT TO FLIP-FLOP <u>STUNTS</u> — 1 GAP CALL RUNNING DOWN & YARDAGE	
53 CALL = MAN-TO-MAN 44 CALL = ZONE	

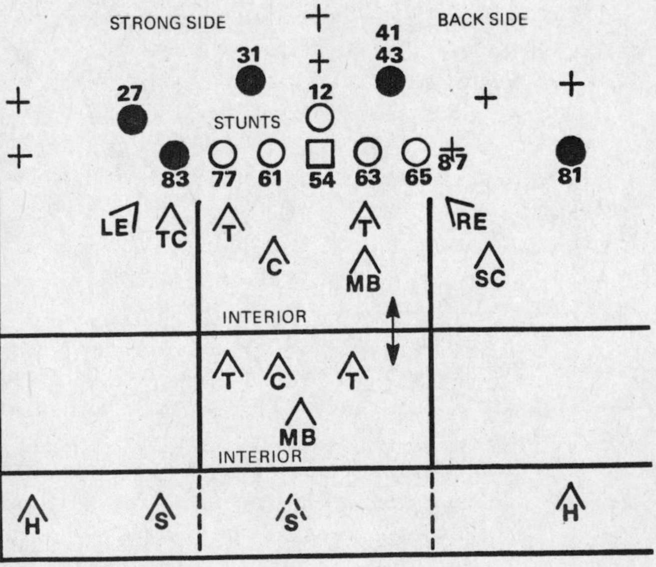

Figure 7-5

8

APPLYING THE COMBO SYSTEM VS. THE WINGED T OFFENSE

The Winged T was a popular offense during the late 50's and early 60's. It was a "T" backfield behind single wing types of blocking. Originally the lines were set tight, heel-to-heel with two tight ends. There are still a number of successful winged T systems around with the split receivers and slots. It is usually a split end to the backside of the formation. Because similiar situations will later appear against some of the more current offensive systems, we will adjust our combo defense against the original winged T systems with two tight ends. Its advantages were that it integrated the speed of the T formation with the power of the single wing, and it increased the problems of adjusting the defenses. Its disadvantages were that it was more difficult to coordinate the speed of the backfield behind the slow development of the power in the line, it doubled the techniques that had to be learned, and it usually resulted in left and right handed tactical tendencies. When their offense is set to their right we will refer to it as our left, and when they are set to their left we will refer to it as our right.

CHARACTERISTICS OF THE WINGED T SYSTEMS

Winged T systems usually make their calls in series, and it is not necessary to number their backs. They combine quick T plays behind dive blocking, and slow developing backfield sequence, or delayed play action series behind post and lead blocking. Post and lead blocking features double team and seal blocks to the inside of the point-of-attack, with pulling linemen and traps to the outside of the holes. There are probably more variations in numbering systems, and backfield sequences with the Winged T, than there are with any other types of offenses. Most Winged T coaches add their own individual innovations, and we will limit ourselves to the coverage of what is commonly wide spread. Some Winged "T" systems flip-flop their whole line to utilize their personnel, while other systems try to run a more balanced

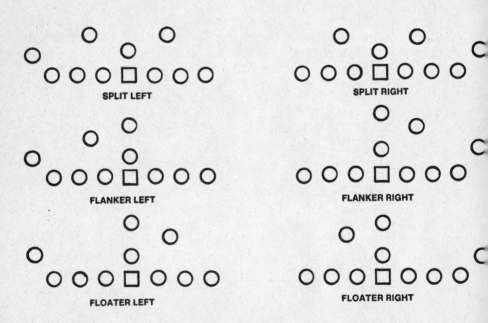

Figure 8-1
Basic Winged T Formations

attack without the flip-flopping lines. Almost all Winged T's flip-flop their backfields.

FIGURE 8-1 shows the six basic formations of the Winged "T" backfield sets. The first two are the split backfields with the Wingbacks' sets to the left and right. The common backfield sequences used with split backfield sets have already been illustrated in Chapter 7. The second two diagrams (Figure 8-1) are backfield sets with the Wingbacks overloaded in a flanker set to the left and right. This leaves a definite left handed or right handed tactical tendency that limits offensive attack to the backside. These have not been popular Wing T sets, because almost all defensive systems can effectively adjust to the flanker side without weakening their positions to the backside.

The last two diagrams (Figure 8-1) are backfield sets with the Wingbacks floating from frontside halfback sets to the left and right. These are the two more popular Wing T formations because the sets place the backfield in positions to present a more balanced attack. Fast halfback and fullback dives, along with delayed backfield sequences behind trap blocking can be run to both the frontside and backside of the formations. The backfield flip-flops behind a balanced line with permanent positions that maintain their same sets. FIGURE 8-2 shows the balance of the basic Winged T sequences run to both the left and the right: There are variations of sweeps, slants, traps up the middle and, wingback counters used for running plays. They feature play action passes to the frontsides, and bootleg run or pass options to the backside. The following descriptions are the plays and their variations in sequence:

1. The first plays of the sequence are slants or sweeps run behind the traps and seals of the two pulling guards. There are two variations of backfield patterns. The first is to fake the fullback trap up the middle before handing-off on a slant. The second is to pitch from a reverse

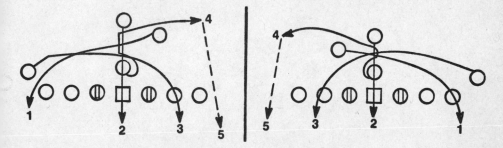

Figure 8-2
Basic Winged T Series

pivot. Both backfield patterns can be run off the wide tackle holes, or wide trying to turn the corners. After the quarterback has either pitched or handed off, he fakes a bootleg in the opposite direction checking out the defense to see if they are staying home.

2. The second plays of the sequence are to hand off to the fullback up the middle behind short traps. After the hand off the quarterback fakes the slants before bootlegging to the backside, and checking out the defense.

3. The third plays of the sequence are Wingback counters run behind the traps and seals of the pulling frontside guards and ends. There are two variations of backfield patterns. The first is to give an outside handoff after faking the slant. The second is for the halfback to make an inside handoff to the Wingback after he has taken a pitch-out from the quarterback. Both backfield patterns can be run over either inside or outside tackle holes. The quarterback's bootleg wide will serve as an influence for the counters that run in the same directions to the inside.

4. The fourth plays of the sequence are the bootlegs. They keep the defenders from the backfield flow from pursuing too fast.

5. The fifth plays of the sequence are the short passes if the quarterback can't run on the bootleg. Bootleg run or pass options are not called until after the defense begins to overreact to the strongsides.

FIGURE 8-3 shows the basic post and lead blocking system used in Winged T offenses. The numbers for the points-of-attack are usually on the offensive linemen instead of the defensive linemen. The post and lead is the

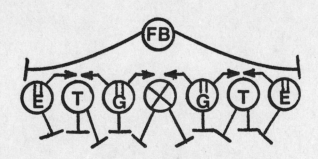

Figure 8-3
Post-Lead Blocking System

double team blocks to the inside of the holes. The holes that are called are soft uncovered spots in the line so that the lead call men will have the blocking angles. The fullbacks and pulling linemen are used to block to the outside of the holes. Frontside guards are used to trap wide, along with backside guards pulling through to seal. Backside guards and ends can be used to trap and seal on off tackle counters. Backside guards or tackles can be used to trap on interior holes. Regardless of the numbering system or blocking rules that are applied to the post and lead, the principles are basically still the same.

ADJUSTING THE COMBO SYSTEM
TO WINGED T TACTICAL TENDENCIES

In order to adjust our defense for sets, keys, and responsibilities, we must take into consideration where the uncovered soft spots are that leave their lead blockers with blocking angles. Their strongside tight end will have the blocking angle on our defensive tackle with both 53 and 44 calls. The offensive guards will have the blocking angles on our combo (noseman) with a 53 call. Because of the angle of their wingback on our defensive end, we will set our split cornerback on the Wingback's side to key him. Our defensive end will still apply his basic technique to meet the play behind their offensive tackle. If the wingback tries to block down on our end, our cornerback comes up fast to meet the play. If this does not work, he can make 5 or 4 gap stunt calls (Figure 5-2). The safety will key and play the tight end man-to-man to the frontside. If he tries to block down on our defensive tackle, our safety will come up fast to fill the hole. Our tight cornerback will apply his bump and recovery techniques on their backside tight end. This will prevent the tight end from blocking down on our tackle to that side, and put our tight cornerback in good position to play the bootleg. The basic techniques of our defensive tackles will force their offensive tackles to our outside preventing them from getting an effective seal on our inside linebackers. Our inside linebackers key the football through their offensive guard for reaction. This will be our basic approach for both 53 and 44 defensive calls.

FIGURES 8-4 and 8-5 show our set adjustments, keys, and responsibilities against the Winged T with both 53 and 44 calls; 53 CALL (Figure 8-4) shows our split cornerback set to our left reading and reacting to their wingback man-to-man. Our safety keys and reacts to their left tight end man-to-man. Our tight cornerback applies his basic bump and recovery technique on their right tight end. Our two halfbacks use zone coverage. The middle linebacker keys the guards and reads the football. If the guard pulls behind his center and the fullback comes, he quickly fills the other guard's hole. If the guard pulls to his outside he goes with him. If a guard comes, he

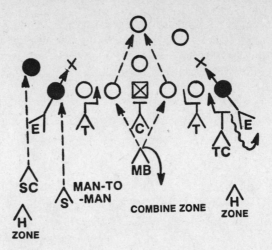

Figure 8-4
53 Call (Combine Zone Man-to-Man)

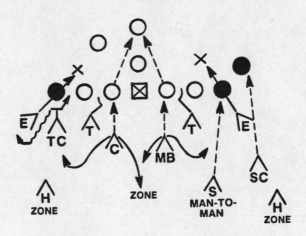

Figure 8-5
44 Call (Combine Zone and Man-To-Man)

goes to meet him. If the guards show pass he covers middle deep (Baker) instead of his regular hook area. 44 CALL (Figure 8-5) shows our split cornerback set to our right reading and reacting to their wingback man-to-man. Our safety keys and reacts to their right tight end man-to-man. Our tight cornerback applies his basic bump and recovery technique on the left tight end. Our two halfbacks use zone coverage. Our two inside linebackers read the football and key their respective defensive guards. If their guard blocks down or comes he meets and fills the hole. If the guard pulls behind his center or shows pass the inside linebacker covers middle deep (Baker). If the guard pulls to the outside he goes with him.

INDIVIDUAL ADJUSTMENTS AGAINST
THE WINGED T RUNNING SEQUENCE

The individual sets, keys, responsibilities, techniques, and reactions are shown and explained for each position against each Winged T play. The 53 calls will be applied in the left panels, and the 44 calls will be applied in the right panels as follows:

FIGURES 8-6 and 8-7 show the halfback slants being run behind the trap and seal of the pulling guards after a fake to the fullback up the middle.

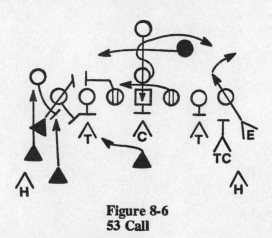

Figure 8-6
53 Call

53 CALL VS. WINGED T SLANT TO OUR LEFT (FIGURE 8-6)

Ends: (both left and right)

1. SETS-Outside and facing through the tight ends.
2. KEYS-Quarterback.
3. RESPONSIBILITIES-Force the play maintaining inside shoulder to the quarterback's playaction.
4. TECHNIQUES-Charge through tight ends sets to positions two yards behind their offensive tackles. Left end should be aware that the wingback has the blocking angle and he must beat him through to that position of control.
5. REACTIONS-The left end meets the pulling guard with his inside

shoulder, and the right end maintains inside shoulder pursuit to the quarterback's bootleg playaction.

Tackles: (both left and right)

1. SETS-Head up, on offensive tackles.
2. KEYS-Fullback and ball.
3. RESPONSIBILITIES-Inside offensive tackle gap.
4. TECHNIQUES-Forearm shiver control on offensive tackle forcing him outside and around, and gaining an inside position of control.
5. REACTIONS-Lateral pursuit angle only after searching the fullback.

Combo: (nose guard)

1. SET-Head up, on offensive center.
2. KEY-Center's hand and ball.
3. RESPONSIBILITIES-Both center and guard gaps.
4. TECHNIQUE-Forearm shiver control on center reading his head.
5. REACTION-Lateral pursuit against pressure.

Middle linebacker:

1. SET-Stacks behind combo.
2. KEY-Read guards through to the football.
3. RESPONSIBILITIES-Lateral pursuit, middle deep (Baker)
4. TECHNIQUE-Play the football.
5. REACTION-Goes with the pulling guards.

Split cornerback:

1. SET-To left side behind and outside heel of his end.
2. KEY-Read wingback man-to-man.
3. RESPONSIBILITIES-If wingback blocks down, he comes up outside to meet the play, and if comes out he picks him up.
4. TECHNIQUE-Dog zone coverage.
5. REACTION-Come up fast to meet the play.

Tight cornerback:

1. SET-To right side, headup on tight end at line of scrimmage in a low two point stance.
2. KEY-Tight end's movement.

3. RESPONSIBILITIES-Force tight end to his outside. Inside control with outside delayed reaction.
4. TECHNIQUE-Forearm shiver on tight end. (Bump and recovery)
5. REACTION-Cover bootleg on recovery.

Safety:

1. SET-6 yards off tight end to our left.
2. KEY-Read left tight end.
3. RESPONSIBILITIES-If the tight end blocks down on our tackle he comes out to fill to his outside, and if he comes out he picks him up.
4. TECHNIQUE-Left hook zone coverage.
5. REACTION-Come up fast to meet the play.

Halfbacks: (both left and right)

Zone: Sets, keys, responsibilities, techniques, and reactions for Charlie and Able respectively.

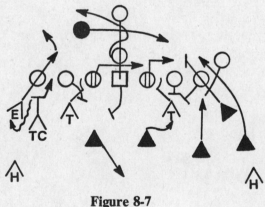

Figure 8-7
44 Call

44 CALL VS. WINGED T SLANT TO OUR RIGHT (FIGURE 8-7)

Ends (both left and right)

1. SETS-Outside and facing through the tight ends.
2. KEYS-Quarterback
3. RESPONSIBILITIES-Force the play maintaining inside shoulder to the quarterback's play action.

4. TECHNIQUES-Charge through tight ends' sets to positions two yards behind their offensive tackles. Right end must be alert to Wingbacks blocking angle.

5. REACTIONS-The left end maintains inside shoulder pursuit to the quarterback's bootleg play action, and the right end meets the pulling guard with his inside shoulder.

Tackles: (both left and right)

1. SETS-Shade inside shoulders of offensive gaps.
2. KEYS-Fullback, football and guards.
3. RESPONSIBILITIES-Inside offensive tackle gap.
4. TECHNIQUES-Forearm shiver reach on offensive guards keeping them off inside linebackers, and gaining the outside position of control.
5. REACTIONS-Lateral pursuit after searching the fullback.

Interior linebackers: (combo and middle linebacker)

1. SETS-Off the offensive guards.
2. KEYS-Read their guards through to the football.
3. RESPONSIBILITIES-Lateral pursuit, middle deep (Baker)
4. TECHNIQUE-Play football
5. REACTIONS-Combo covers Baker, and middle linebacker goes with pulling guard.

Split cornerback

1. SET-To right side, behind and outside heel of his end.
2. KEY-Read Wingback.
3. RESPONSIBILITIES-If the wingback blocks down he comes up to meet the play, and if he comes out he picks him up.
5. TECHNIQUE-Easy zone coverage.
5. REACTION-Comes up fast to outside.

Tight cornerback

1. SET-To left side, head-up on tight end at L.O.S. in a low two point stance.
2. KEY-Tight end's movement.
3. RESPONSIBILITIES-Force tight end's delay to his outside. Inside control with outside delayed reaction.
4. TECHNIQUE-Bump and recovery.
5. REACTION-Cover bootleg on recovery.

Safety

1. SET-6 yards off tight end to our right.
2. KEY-Read right tight end.
3. RESPONSIBILITIES-If tight end trys to block down come up and fill to his outside. And if he comes out pick him up.
4. TECHNIQUE-Right hook zone coverage.
5. REACTION-Come up fast to meet the play.

Half backs (both left and right)

Zone: Sets, keys, responsibilities, techniques, and reactions for Able and Charlie.

FIGURE 8-8 and 8-9 show the fullback trap being run up the middle followed by faking the slant with bootleg playaction. The sets, keys, responsibilities, and techniques, for all positions remain basically the same as in Figure 8-5. The only variations are the final reactions to the differences in the plays. We will only cover the reactions of each position to the plays to prevent repetition. This affects the interior defensive front.

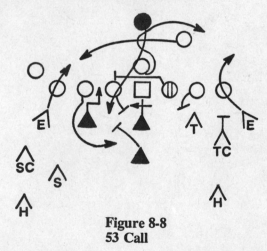

Figure 8-8
53 Call

53 CALL VS. WINGED T FULLBACK TRAP TO OUR LEFT (FIGURE 8-8)

ENDS: Basically the same.
CORNERBACKS: Basically the same
HALFBACKS: Basically the same.
SAFETY: Basically the same
TACKLES: (Both left and right)

1. Left tackle's technique forces the offensive tackle to his outside to prevent him from getting a seal angle on the middle linebacker. His reaction must be to close down quickly on the pulling guard who is to trap him.
2. Right tackle's reaction is to close down quickly from the backside.

COMBO: Reacts to left pressure from his control position on the center to stablizes the lead block of the offensive guard.

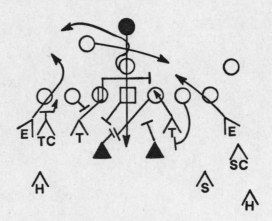

Figure 8-9
44 Call

44 CALL VS. WINGED T FULLBACK TRAP TO OUR RIGHT (FIGURE 8-9)

Again the reactions of the ends, cornerbacks, halfbacks, and safety are basically the same as they were in Figures 8-6 and 8-7. Our interior front presents four defensive players on three offensive players which should shut down the middle.

TACKLES: (both left and right)

1. *Left tackle's* reaction should be to follow through on his reach technique which should place him in a position to make the tackle from the backside.
2. *Right tackle's* reaction should be to follow through on his reach technique which should place him in a position to close down on the pulling guard trying to trap him.

COMBO'S reaction should put him in position to meet the seal based on his key.

MIDDLE LINEBACKER'S REACTION should put him in position to fill the hole based on his key.

FIGURES 8-10 and 8-11 show the wingbacked counters being run behind the trap and seal of the respective pulling guards and tight ends. Again the sets, keys, responsibilities, and techniques for all positions are basically the same. Their following reactions to the counters should and will vary based on their keys.

53 CALL VS. WINGED T WINGBACK COUNTER
TO OUR RIGHT (FIGURE 8-10)

LEFT END'S Reaction should be to follow the wingback and pulling tight end, and make the tackle from behind since the quarterback will bootleg to the right.

RIGHT END'S Reaction should be to close down on the outside shoulder of the pulling guard and cover the quarterback's bootleg playaction to the right. After contact.

LEFT TACKLE'S Reaction should be a right pursuit angle.

RIGHT TACKLE'S Reaction should be a right lateral pursuit.

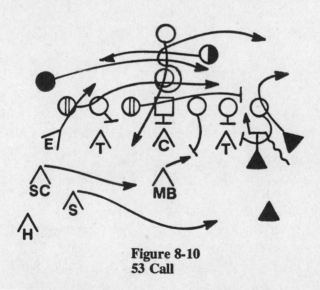

Figure 8-10
53 Call

COMBO'S Reaction should be a right lateral pursuit.

MIDDLE LINEBACKER'S Reaction should be right lateral movement with offensive guard pulling behind his center.

TIGHT CORNERBACK'S Reaction should be to fill the hole after he has forced the right tight end to the outside destroying his angle for a lead block.

SPLIT CORNERBACK'S Reaction should be lateral pursuit to the right with their wingback.

SAFETY'S Reaction should be lateral pursuit to the right with their pulling tight end.

LEFT HALF'S Reaction should be to stay home.

RIGHT HALF'S Reaction should be an outside deep containment.

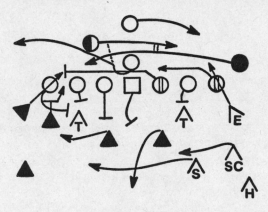

Figure 8-11
44 Call

44 CALL VS. WINGED T WINGBACK COUNTER TO OUR LEFT (FIGURE 8-11)

LEFT END'S Reaction should be to close down on the outside shoulder of the pulling guard and cover the quarterback's bootleg playaction to the left after contact.

RIGHT END'S Reaction should be to follow the wingback and pulling tight end, and make the tackle from behind since the quarterback will bootleg to the left.

LEFT TACKLE'S Reaction should be gap penetration.

RIGHT TACKLE'S Reaction should be a left pursuit angle.

COMBO'S Reaction should be a left lateral movement.

MIDDLE LINEBACKER'S Reaction should be middle deep (Baker) zone coverage.

TIGHT CORNERBACK'S Reaction should be to fill the hole after he has forced the left tight end to the outside destroying his angle for a lead block.

SPLIT CORNERBACK'S reaction should be lateral pursuit to the left with their wingback.

SAFETY'S Reaction should be a lateral pursuit to the left with their pulling tight end.

LEFT HALF'S Reaction should be an outside deep containment.

RIGHT HALF'S Reaction should be at home.

We have shown both 53 and 44 defenses against the Winged T offense. A 44 alignment is our primary defensive call, and we only use the 53 alignments as a supplementary call because of offensive tactical tendencies. We will conclude with the reasons for this after we have covered the secondary adjustments.

SECONDARY ADJUSTMENTS AGAINST THE WINGED T PASSING GAME

The Winged T uses a combination of play action and bootleg passes. This means our secondary must not overreact. Usually we apply either straight zone or man-to-man coverage. Because of the tactical tendencies of their running game we need to free our safety from zone to man-to-man coverage. Because of their bootleg threat, our halfbacks need to stay home with outside deep zone containment. This means that our three deep will be applying a combination of zone and man-to-man coverage. Our interior linebackers will be covering the middle deep (Baker) Zone based on keys.

Our ends and tackles apply their basic containments and pass rush. The sets, keys, responsibilities, techniques, and reactions of each position of our pass defenders will be covered. These positions are: The two halfbacks, safety, split cornerback, tight cornerback, combo, and middle linebacker.

FIGURES 8-12 and 8-13 show playaction passes being run against our 53 defense to the left, and against our 44 defense to the right.

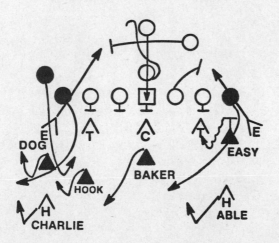

Figure 8-12
53 Call

53 CALL VS. WINGED T PLAYACTION PASS
TO OUR LEFT (FIGURE 8-12)

Halfbacks: (both left and right)

1. SETS-10 to 12 yards, outside deep zones.
2. KEYS-Outside receivers (flanker and split end).
3. RESPONSIBILITIES-Charlie and Able zones respectively.
4. TECHNIQUES Zones.
5. REACTIONS-To deep receivers in their zones.

Safety:

1. SET-6 yards off the tight end to our left.
2. KEY-Read the left tight end man-to-man.
3. RESPONSIBILITIES-Left hook zone. If tight end crosses over the middle, cover him man-to-man to the right hook zone.
4. TECHNIQUE-Basically man-to-man.
5. REACTION-Covers wingback in left hook zone.

Split cornerback:

1. SET-To left side, behind outside heel of his end.
2. KEY-Read wingback man-to-man.
3. RESPONSIBILITIES-Left dog zone coverage.
4. TECHNIQUE-Basically man-to-man.
5. REACTION-Covers tight end in left flat.

Tight cornerback:

1. SET-On right tight end in a low two point stance.
2. KEY-Tight end's movement.
3. RESPONSIBILITIES-Force tight end's delay to his outside, and cover Easy.
4. TECHNIQUE-Bump and recovery.
5. REACTION-Stay home (Easy).

Middle linebacker:

1. SET-Stacked behind middle guard.
2. KEY-Read football through guards.
3. RESPONSIBILITIES-Middle deep passes.
4. TECHNIQUE-Zone coverage.
5. REACTION-Sprint to Baker.

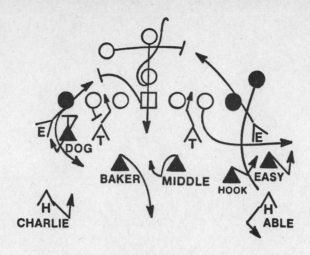

Figure 8-13
44 Call

44 CALL VS. WINGED T PLAYACTION PASS
TO OUR RIGHT HALFBACKS: (BOTH LEFT AND RIGHT)
SAME AS 53 CALL (FIGURE 8-13)

Safety:

1. SET-6 yards off the tight end to right.
2. KEY-Read the right tight end man-to-man.
3. RESPONSIBILITIES-Right hook zone. If tight end crosses over the middle, cover him man-to-man to the left hook zone.
4. TECHNIQUE-Basically man-to-man.
5. REACTIONS-Check tight end and wingback cover right hook.

Split cornerback:

1. SET-To right side, behind outside heel of his end.
2. KEY-Read wingback man-to-man.
3. RESPONSIBILITIES-Right easy zone coverage.
4. TECHNIQUE-Basically man-to-man.
5. REACTION-Covers tight end in right flat.

Tight cornerback:

1. SET-On left tight end in a low two point stance.
2. KEY-Tight end's movement

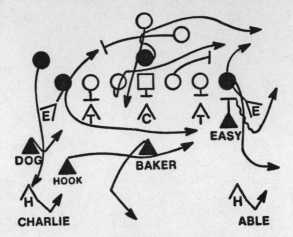

Figure 8-14
53 Call

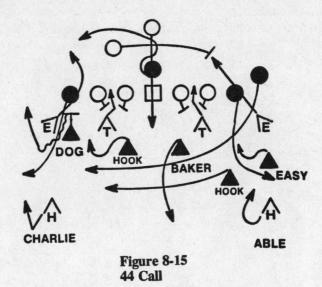

Figure 8-15
44 Call

3. RESPONSIBILITIES-Force tight end's delay to his outside and cover Dog.
4. TECHNIQUE-Bump and recovery.
5. REACTION-Stay home (Dog).

Interior linebackers: (combo and middle linebacker)

1. SETS-Head up and off respective guards.
2. KEYS-Read football through guards.

3. RESPONSIBILITIES-Hooks, middle, or deep Baker.
4. TECHNIQUES-Zone coverage.
5. REACTIONS-Combo Baker and MLB-Middle.

The bootleg pass run option is only effective if the pass defenders over-react to flow of offense and don't stay home. If they maintain their basic assignments, their reactions should put them in natural positions to contain the bootleg.

FIGURES 8-14 and 8-15 show bootleg passes being run against our 53 defense to the left, and against our 44 defense to the right.

53 CALL (Figure 8-14) The tight cornerback and right end should be in good positions to pursue the quarterback's bootleg action. The safety picks up the left tight end and covers him man-to-man to the right hook area.

44 CALL (Figure 8-15) We have the same situation to the left except the combo gives us additional hook coverage to the backside.

This gives us two reasons for using the 44 call as our primary defense, and the 53 call our supplementary defense against a winged T offense. First: The interior defensive alignments are more effective against the running attack, with the aid of our free safety. Second: Two interior linebackers gives us one for basic coverage, and the other for middle deep zone coverage which was normally the safety's responsibility.

9

PLAYING THE COMBO DEFENSE AGAINST THE SLOT I

The I formations were an outgrowth of the Winged T, and became a popular offense during the late 60's. The tailback was in a good position from his deep set in a two point stance to take a hand-off, and read his blocks. Isolation blocking was applied, which combined speed and power techniques. Its advantages are good timing in the coordination of backfield and line, and it is a good alignment for shifting with fast deployment to Winged T backfield sets. It is currently one of the more popular formations used in football. Its disadvantages are that it has a tactical tendency to overuse the tailback behind the blocking of the fullback. Even when a fullback belly sequence is utilized in the attack, misdirection counters or cross action plays are required to prevent the fullback from leading the defense to the flow of the plays.

CHARACTERISTICS OF THE I OFFENSIVE SYSTEMS

I systems usually make their calls in series without numbering their backs. They combine quick fullback sequence plays behind dive blocking, and tailback reading behind isolation blocking. Isolation blocking features blocks of defensive linemen on the line-of-scrimmage to the outside and inside of a hole. The point-of-attack is usually the soft uncovered spot between these blocks, with a blocking back leading the reading tailback through the hole.

FIGURE 9-1 shows the six basic formations of the I backfield sets. The first two are the fullhouse power I backfield sets to the left and right. They are popular in short yardage or goal line situations.

The second two diagrams (Figure 9-1) are the backfields flanked left and right behind the pro set lines. These are more often used with the shifts to T formation backfield sets for the fast deployment of flip-flopping personnel.

The last two diagrams (Figure 9-1) are the slot I backfields set to both the left and right. These are the more common and popular alignments of the I formations. The sets place the backfield in positions to present a more balanced attack. The slot can be quickly utilized as a blocker, receiver, or counter action ball carrier. Fullback dive plays, and tailback isolation or cross

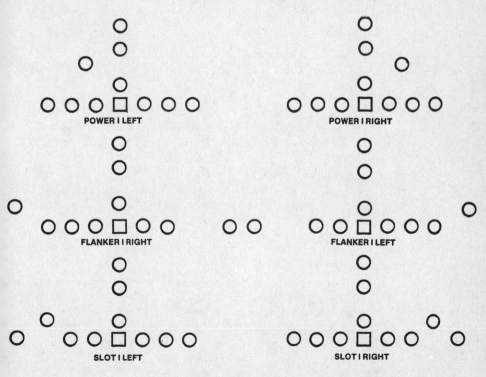

Figure 9-1
Basic I Formations

traps can be run to both the frontsides and backsides of the formations. A combination of straight on, isolation, and pulling linemen can be used for blocking. The quarterback usually lead steps with fullback sequences, and reverse pivots with tailback plays. A large variety of techniques can be applied.

FIGURE 9-2 shows the balance of the basic Slot I sequences run to both the left and right. There are variations of tailback isolations or cross traps, fullback dives with options, and slot counters used for running plays. They feature play action and sprint out passes.

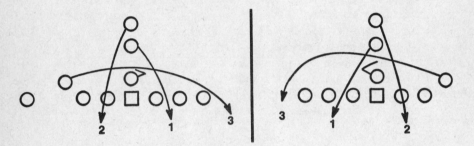

Figure 9-2
Basic Slot I Series

1. The first plays of the sequence are the fullback bellies with options to the tailback or slotback in motion run behind dive blocking. This series can be run to both the frontside and backside. The quarterback usually lead steps.

2. The second plays of the sequence are the tailback following his fullback through the hole behind isolation blocking, and the tailback taking a counter hand off behind trap blocking after a fake to the fullback. With the tailback isolations, the quarterback can either lead step or reverse pivot. With the tailback cross trap the quarterback lead steps on his fake to the fullback, and then reverse pivots for his hand off to the tailback.

3. The third plays of the sequence are slotback counters behind the trap and seal of both pulling guards. There are two variations of backfield patterns. The first is to take an outside hand off after faking the tailback isolations, and the second is to take an outside hand off after faking the tailback cross trap.

FIGURE 9-3 shows the basic isolation blocking system used with I offenses. The numbers for points-of-attack can either be on the offensive or defensive linemen. The holes are called over an uncovered offensive lineman

Figure 9-3
Basic Slot I Isolation Blocking System

who can block the near linebacker. The offensive linemen to the inside and outside of the call block the defensive linemen on the line-of-scrimmage in and out respectively. The fullback or slotback can lead the ball carrier through the hole. Figure 9-3 illustrates the relationships between blocking angles, lead blocks, and paths of the ball carrier.

ADJUSTING THE COMBO SYSTEM
TO SLOT I TACTICAL TENDENCIES

In order to adjust our defense for sets, keys, and responsibilities, we must take into consideration where the uncovered soft spots are for their isolation blocks. Their backside is the tightside, and only their guard can be considered as a soft spot in both our 53 and 44 alignments. Since he cannot be released on our linebacker we can play it basically straight. Their frontside to the slot is the split side, and all their offensive linemen have blocking angles against both our 53 and 44 alignments. Because of this we will need to penetrate the split side with stunt calls. Our split cornerback and defensive end will apply 5 or 4 gap calls on 53 alignments, and our stacked interior linebacker and tackle will apply 3 or 2 gap call on 44 alignments. Anytime that we are stunting these areas we will use man-to-man coverage. The half-back will key their respective ends, and the safety will key their slot back. This should put our defensive alignments in positions to get a number of defensive players to the right places in a hurry in reacting to the offensive plays. This will be our basic approaches for our 53 and 44 defensive calls.

FIGURES 9-4 and 9-5 show our set adjustments, keys, and responsibilities against the Slot I with both 53 and 44 calls.

53 CALL (Figure 9-4) shows our split cornerback set to our left reading and reacting to their slot back. Our safety also sets to our left, and keys and

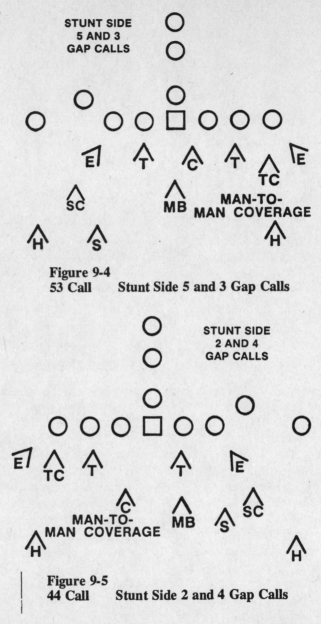

Figure 9-4
53 Call   Stunt Side 5 and 3 Gap Calls

Figure 9-5
44 Call   Stunt Side 2 and 4 Gap Calls

reacts to their slot back. Our right cornerback applies his basic bump and recovery technique on their right tight end. Our two halfbacks use zone coverage on the basic 53 call, and man-to-man coverage on a 5 gap stunt. The middle linebacker keys the guard, and reads the football. If the guard pulls behind his center he quickly fills the other guard's hole. If the guard pulls to his outside he goes with him. If a guard comes, he goes to meet him, and if they show pass he covers the left hook area. The tackles and combo apply their basic techniques from their basic alignments. 44 CALL (Figure 9-5) shows our split cornerback set to our right reading and reacting to their slot back. Our safety also sets to our right, and keys and reacts to their slot back. Our tight cornerback applies his basic bump and recovery technique on their left tight end. Our two halfbacks use zone coverage on the basic 44 call, and man-to-man coverage on a 2 gap stunt. The interior front applies their basic 44 split side and tight side alignments and techniques. The two interior linebackers cover their respective hook areas on passes.

INDIVIDUAL ADJUSTMENTS AGAINST
THE SLOT I RUNNING SEQUENCE

The individual sets, keys, responsibilities, techniques, and reactions are shown and explained for each position against each Slot I play. The 53 calls will be applied to our left, and the 44 calls will be applied to our right as follows:

FIGURES 9-6 and 9-7 show the fullback belly with option series being run to our tight sides.

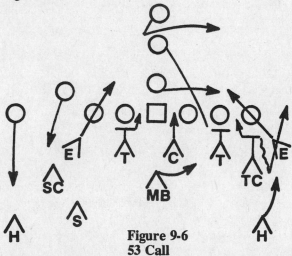

Figure 9-6
53 Call

53 Call vs. fullback series to our right (Figure 9-6)
  LEFT END:

1. SET-Outside and facing through tackle.
2. KEY-Quarterback.
3. RESPONSIBILITIES-Force the play maintaining inside shoulder to quarterback's play action.

4. TECHNIQUE-Charge through the set of their left tackle beating the slot back to the position two yards behind the tackle.

5. REACTION-Trail the quarterback being alert for a counter hand-off.

RIGHT END:

1. SET-Outside and facing through tight end.
2. KEY-Quarterback.
3. RESPONSIBILITIES-Force the play maintaining inside shoulder on quarterback and a fast pitch on the option.
4. TECHNIQUE-Charge through tight end's set to a position two yards behind tackle.
5. REACTION-Hit the quarterback with inside shoulder.

LEFT TACKLE:

1. SET-Head up, on left guard.
2. KEY-Ball and fullback.
3. RESPONSIBILITIES-Inside guard gap.
4. TECHNIQUE-Forearm shiver control.
5. REACTION-Lateral pursuit.

RIGHT TACKLE:

1. SET-Head up, on right tackle.
2. KEY-Ball and fullback.
3. RESPONSIBILITIES-Inside tackle gap.
4. TECHNIQUE-Forearm shiver control.
5. REACTION-Tackle and fullback.

COMBO:

1. SET-Center and right guard gap to tight side.
2. KEY-Center's hand and ball.
3. RESPONSIBILITIES-The gap.
4. TECHNIQUE-Shoot the gap.
5. REACTION-Grab legs.

MIDDLE LINEBACKER:

1. SET-Over the center and off the L.O.S.
2. KEY-Read guards through to the tailback.
3. RESPONSIBILITIES-Holes between tackles.

4. TECHNIQUE-Play the football.

5. REACTION-Goes with quarterback and fullback.

SPLIT CORNERBACK:

1. SET-Triangles left split.

2. KEY-Read slot back.

3. RESPONSIBILITIES-If slot back blocks down, he comes up outside to meet the play, and if he comes out he picks him up.

4. TECHNIQUE-Dog zone coverage.

5. REACTION-Stay home.

TIGHT CORNERBACK:

1. SET-To right side, head-up on tight end at line-of-scrimmage in a low two point stance.

2 KEY-Tight end's movement.

3. RESPONSIBILITIES-Force tight end to his outside. Inside control, with outside delay reaction.

4. TECHNIQUE-Bump and recovery.

REACTION-Pitchout from option.

SAFETY:

1. SET-6 to 8 yards off slot back to our left.

2. KEY-Read left slot back.

3. RESPONSIBILITIES-If slot back blocks down, he comes up, and if he comes out he covers Baker.

4. TECHNIQUE-Zone coverage.

5. REACTION-Rotate to Baker.

HALFBACKS: (both left and right)

Zone coverage on basic 53 call, and man-to-man coverage on a 5 or 4 stunt gap call.

44 Call vs. fullback series to our left (Figure 9-7)

LEFT END:

1. SET-Outside facing through tight end.

2. KEY-Quarterback.

3. RESPONSIBILITIES-When tight end blocks out on him, he automatically has the outside.

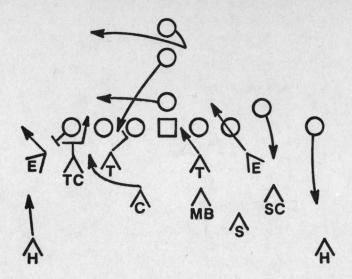

Figure 9-7
44 Call

4. TECHNIQUE-Control after contact.
5. REACTION-Outside lateral pursuit.

RIGHT END:

1. SET-Outside facing through tackle.
2. KEY-Quarterback.
3. RESPONSIBILITIES-Force play maintaining an inside shoulder to quarterback.
4. TECHNIQUE-Charge through tackle's set to a position two yards behind him.
5. REACTION-Trail the quarterback being alert for a counter hand-off.

LEFT TACKLE:

1. SET-Shade inside shoulder of offensive tackle.
2. KEY-Ball and fullback.
3 RESPONSIBILITIES-Inside tackle gap.
4. TECHNIQUE-Forearm shiver reach on offensive guard.
5. REACTION-Tackle fullback.

RIGHT TACKLE:

1. SET-Head on offensive guard.
2. KEY-Ball and fullback.
3. RESPONSIBILITIES-Inside tackle gap.
4. TECHNIQUE-Forearm shiver, read the head.
5. REACTION-Pursuit.

COMBO:

1. SET-Over the left guard and off the L.O.S.
2. KEY-Left guard through to the tailback.
3. RESPONSIBILITIES-Holes between left tackle and center.
4. TECHNIQUE-Play the football.
5. REACTION-Fill outside tackle hole.

MIDDLE LINEBACKER:

1. SET-Stacked behind his tackle.
2. KEY-Right guard through tailback.
3. RESPONSIBILITIES-Holes between center and right tackle.
4. TECHNIQUE-Play the football.
5. REACTION-Back up Combo.

SPLIT CORNERBACKER:

1. SET-Triangles right split.
2. KEY-Reads right slot back.
3. RESPONSIBILITIES-If slot back blocks down, he comes up outside to meet the play, and if he comes he picks him up.
4. TECHNIQUE-Easy zone coverage.
5. REACTION-Stay home.

TIGHT CORNERBACK:

1. SET-To left side, head up on tight end at L.O.S. in a low two point stance.
2. KEY-Tight end's movement.
3. RESPONSIBILITIES-Force tight end to his outside, with inside control.
4. TECHNIQUE-Bump and control.
5. REACTION-When tight end tries to block the end, he penetrates forcing the quarterback on a quick pitch from the option.

SAFETY:

1. SET-6 to 8 yards off slot back to our right.
2. KEY-Reads right slot back.
3. RESPONSIBILITIES-If slot back blocks down, he comes up outside to meet the play, and if he comes up pick him up.
4. TECHNIQUE-Zone coverage.
5. REACTION-Rotate to Baker.

HALFBACKS: (BOTH LEFT AND RIGHT)

Zone coverage on basic 44 call, and man-to-man coverage on a 3 or 2 stunt gap calls.

FIGURES 9-8 and 9-9 show the tailback isolation being run against a 53 defense to our left, and the tailback cross counter being run against a 44 defense to our right. The sets, keys, responsibilities, and techniques for all positions remain basically the same as in Figures 9-6 and 9-7. The only variations are the final reactions to the difference in the plays. We will only cover the reactions of each position to the plays to prevent repetition.

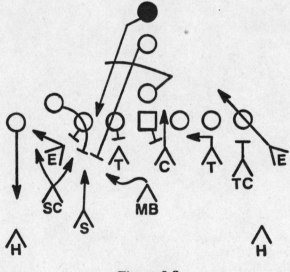

Figure 9-8
53 Call

53 Call vs. tailback isolation to our left (Figure 9-8)

LEFT END: Outside lateral pursuit as a result of tight end blocking out.

RIGHT END: Basically the same.
SPLIT CORNERBACK: Fill the hole as a result of the slot back leading through the hole.
TIGHT CORNERBACK: Basically the same.
LEFT TACKLE: React to pressure.
RIGHT TACKLE: Basically the same.
COMBO: Basically the same.
MIDDLE LINEBACKER: React to the play.
SAFETY: Fill the hole based on slot backs lead through the hole.
HALFBACKS: Basically the same.

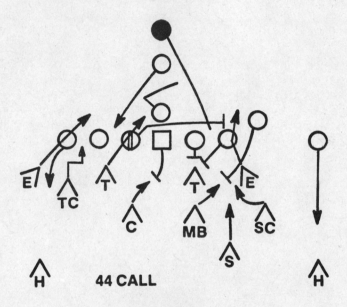

44 CALL

Figure 9-9
44 Call

44 Call vs. tailback cross trap to our right (Figure 9-9)

LEFT END: Basically the same.
RIGHT END: Close down on trap.
LEFT TACKLE: As a result of reach technique on pulling guard get the play from behind.
RIGHT TACKLE: Fight pressure.
COMBO: Back up middle linebacker after reaction to fullback.
MIDDLE LINEBACKER: React to tailback.
SAFETY: Fill the hole based on seal block of the slot back.
HALFBACKS: Basically the same.

FIGURES 9-10 and 9-11 show the slot back counter being run to our right after faking the tailback cross against our 53 defense, and the slot back counter being run to our left after faking the tailback isolation against our 44 defense. Both counters are run behind the traps and seals of the pulling guards. Again the sets, keys, responsibilities, and technique for all positions are basically the same. Their following reactions to the counters will vary based on their keys.

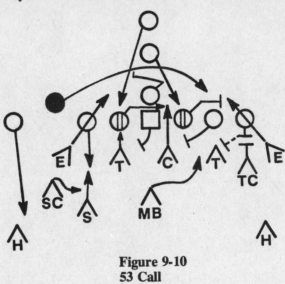

Figure 9-10
53 Call

53 Call vs. slotback cross counter to our right (Figure 9-10)

LEFT END: Basically the same.
RIGHT END: Close down on trap.
LEFT TACKLE: Penetrate with pulling guard.
RIGHT TACKLE: React to pressure.
COMBO: Penetrate with pulling guard.
MIDDLE LINEBACKER: Right pursuit based on keys.
TIGHT CORNERBACK: Outside recovery.
SPLIT CORNERBACK: Pursuit right with slotback.
SAFETY: Rotate right to Baker.
LEFT HALF: Reaction should be to stay at home.
RIGHT HALF: Outside deep containment.

44 Call vs. slotback counter to our left (Figure 9-11)

LEFT END: Close down on trap.
RIGHT END: Basically the same.
LEFT TACKLE: React to pressure.

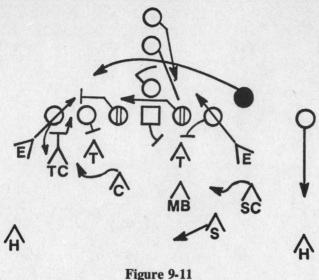

Figure 9-11
44 Call

RIGHT TACKLE: Penetrate with pulling guard.
COMBO: Fill outside tackle hole based on key of pulling left guard.
MIDDLE LINEBACKER: Back-up combo based on key of pulling
    right guard.
TIGHT CORNERBACK: Outside recovery.
SPLIT CORNERBACK: Pursuit left with slotback.
SAFETY: Rotate left to Baker.
LEFT HALF: Outside deep containment.
RIGHT HALF: Stay at home.

This completes the adjustments of both 53 and 44 defenses against the basic running attack of the slot I offense. Next we will show the adjustments against the passing attack.

SECONDARY ADJUSTMENTS AGAINST
THE SLOT I PASSING GAME

Most Slot I systems use a playaction or sprintout passing attack. The playaction passes can either be a fake to the tailback or fullback. The sprintout or sprintback puts quick pressure on the secondary. We use man-to-man coverage with our stunt calls. With our basic 53 and 44 defense our three deep will apply zone coverage. Our interior linebackers will cover the hook areas, and our two corner backs will cover the short flats.

Our ends and tackles apply their basic containments and pass rush. The sets, keys, responsibilities, techniques, and reactions of each position of our pass defenders will be covered. These positions are: The two halfbacks, safety, split cornerback, tight cornerback, combo, and middle linebacker.

FIGURES 9-12 and 9-13 show a tailback playaction pass being run to the left against our 53 defense, and a sprintback pass being run to the right against our 44 defense:

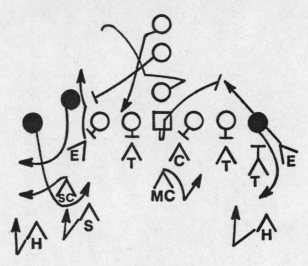

Figure 9-12
53 Call

53 Call vs. slot I playaction pass to our left (Figure 9-12)

HALFBACKS: (BOTH LEFT AND RIGHT)

1. SETS-10 to 12 yards, outside deep zones.
2. KEYS-Outside receivers (split and tight ends).
3. RESPONSIBILITIES-Charlie and Able zones respectively.
4. TECHNIQUES-Zone coverage.
5. REACTIONS-Deep receivers in their zones.

SAFETY:

1. SET-6 yards off slot back to our left.
2. KEY-Read the left slot back.
3. RESPONSIBILITIES-Baker zone rotation.
4. TECHNIQUE-Basically man-to-man.
5. REACTION-Behind hook of split end.

SPLIT CORNERBACK:

1. SET-Triangles left split.
2. KEY-Read left slot back.
3. RESPONSIBILITIES-Outside Dog zone.
4. TECHNIQUE-Basically man-to-man.
5. REACTION-Covers slotback in left flat.

TIGHT CORNERBACK:

1. SET-On right tight end in a low two point stance.
2. KEY-Tight end's movement.
3. RESPONSIBILITIES-Force tight end's delay to his outside, and covers Easy.
4. TECHNIQUE-Bump and recovery.
5. REACTION-Covers Easy zone.

MIDDLE LINEBACKER:

1. SET-Over the center and off the L.O.S.
2. KEY-Reads football through center.
3. RESPONSIBILITIES-Left hook area.
4. TECHNIQUE-Zone coverage.
5. REACTION-Left front of split end's hook.

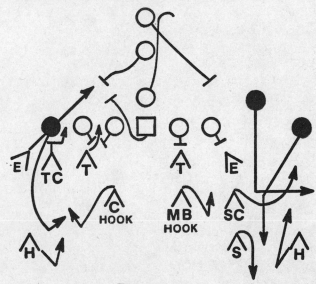

Figure 9-13
44 Call

44 Call vs. slot I sprintback pass to our right (Figure 9-13)

HALFBACKS: (BOTH LEFT AND RIGHT) Same as 53 call.

SAFETY:

1. SET-6 yards off the slot back to right.
2. KEY-Read the right slot back.
3. RESPONSIBILITIES-Baker zone rotation.
4 TECHNIQUE-Basically man-to-man.
5. REACTION-Picks up split end in Baker.

SPLIT CORNERBACK:

1. SET-Triangles right split.
2. KEY-Read right slot back.
3. RESPONSIBILITIES-Outside Easy zone.
4. TECHNIQUE-Basically man-to-man.
5. REACTION-Covers slot back in right flat.

TIGHT CORNERBACK:

1. SET-On left tight end in low two point stance.
2. KEY-Tight end's movement.
3. RESPONSIBILITIES-Force tight end's delay to his outside, and covers Dog.
4. TECHNIQUE-Bump and recovery.
5. REACTION-Covers Dog zone.

COMBO:

1. SET-Over the left guard and off the L.O.S.
2. KEY-Reads football through left guard.
3. RESPONSIBILITIES-Left hook area.
4 TECHNIQUE-Zone coverage.
5. REACTION-Left front of tight end's hook.

MIDDLE LINEBACKER:

1. SET-Stacked behind his left tackle.
2. KEY-Read football through right guard.
3. RESPONSIBILITIES-Right hook area.
4. TECHNIQUE-Zone coverage.
5. REACTION-Right hook pursuit.

If we run into a Power I we use the same alignment adjustments as we would against a Winged T (Chapter 8). Our pass defenders would make similar adjustments as they would against a Wishbone (Chapter 10). If we run into an I formation with a pro-set in the line we would use the same alignments and adjustments we use against the basic veer formations (Chapter 11) with split backfields.

10

HOW TO USE THE COMBO
SYSTEM AGAINST
THE WISHBONE

The Wishbone offense was an outgrowth of the Split T (fullback belly), and became a popular offense during the early 70's. It features the triple option, and both terms are household words today. It has caused a lot of changes and adjustments in defenses. The big differences from the old fullback belly series are the first option on the defensive tackle for the fullback, the pitchout has priority over the quarterback keep, a lead blocker out of the backfield, and the offensive tackle or end do not block on the line of scrimmage at the points-of-attack. Its advantages are a devastating running attack, and simple for the players to understand. The disadvantages are limitations in the alignments for a passing attack, requires a lot of time to perfect techniques, and needs above average personnel. The triple option being run from the Wishbone needs a well schooled quarterback, a hard running fullback, and two fast running halfbacks.

CHARACTERISTICS OF THE WISHBONE OFFENSE

The Wishbone is based on the "KISS" approach. This is to "keep it short and simple" or "Keep it simple stupid." It is based on a philosophy to learn to do but a few things well. The Wishbone systems usually number their backs to designate ball carriers, and number the defensive players to determine blocking assignments. This is more of a carry over from tradition, instead of a result of function. Actually, the numbering systems do not make that much of a difference. Since the offensive linemen at the point-of-attacks do not have to block on the line-of-scrimmage, they can be utilized in a variety of ways. They can pull to influence or lead the plays wide, or they can block the linebackers off the line of scrimmage. Power plays from the fullhouse backfield of the Wishbone are usually integrated along with the triple option series. Either isolation or tandem blocks are applied.

FIGURE 10-1 shows the basic Wishbone formations. Since the fullback's set is much closer to the line-of-scrimmage than the sets of the halfbacks, the fullhouse backfield alignment takes on the appearance of a Wishbone. The backfield is set behind a line with a split end to one side, and a tight end to the other. The left panel illustrates the split set to our left, and the right panel illustrates the split set to our right.

Figure 10-1
Basic Wishbone Formations

FIGURE 10-2 shows the triple option sequences run to both the left and right split sides and tight sides:

Their left split side series shows the first option being run with the outside fullback slant to our left. The second option is the quarterback keep. The third option is the pitchout to the right halfback behind the lead blocks of the left halfback and split end. (Top, left diagram)

Their right split side series shows the first option being run with the outside fullback slant to our right. The second option is the quarterback keep. The third option is the pitchout to the left halfback behind the lead blocks of the right halfback and split end. (Top, right diagram)

Their left tight side series shows the first option being run with the inside fullback belly to our right. The second option is the quarterback keep. The

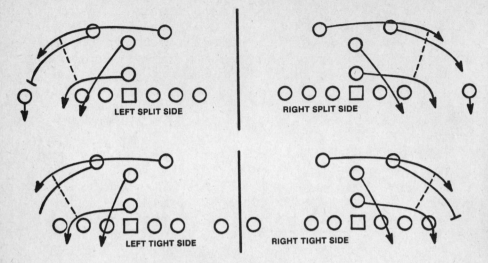

Figure 10-2
Basic Wishbone Series (Triple Option)

third option is the pitchout to the right halfback behind the lead block of the left halfback. (Bottom, left diagram)

Their right tightside series shows the first option being run with the inside fullback belly to our right. The second option is the quarterback keep. The third option is the pitchout to the left halfback behind the lead block of the right halfback. (Bottom, right diagram)

FIGURE 10-3 shows the basic blocking system used with the triple option. The tackle and end are released to block the near linebackers, or pull and lead the plays wide since the options are basically being made off of the defensive tackles and ends. There are many blocking variations, and we will illustrate only the basic possibilities.

The left split side shows their tackle blocking the left defensive tackle for the outside fullback slant. This results in all three options being run off the left defensive end. (Top, left panel)

The right split side shows their guard blocking the right tackle, and their tackle on the right inside linebacker. This results in the first option being run off the right defensive end, and the second or third options being run off the right cornerback. (Top, right panel)

The left tight side shows their tackle being released to block on the left interior linebacker, and their tight end either releasing or pulling to block off the line-of-scrimmage. This results in the first option being run inside the defensive left tackle, and the second or third options being run off the defensive left end. (Bottom, left panel)

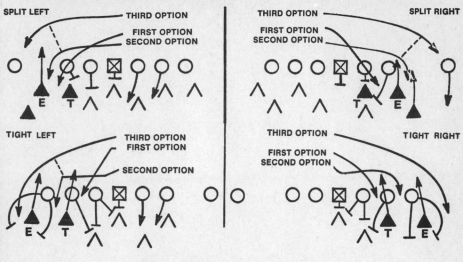

Figure 10-3
Triple Option Blocking System

The right tight side shows their tackle being released to block the right interior linebacker, and their tight end either pulling or being released to block off the line-of-scrimmage. This results in their first option being run to the inside of the defensive right tackle, and their second and third options being run off on the defensive end. (Bottom, right panel)

Regardless if the offensive linemen pull or release to block off the line-of-scrimmage, or which defensive down linemen the options are keyed, the principles are basically the same.

ADJUSTING THE COMBO SYSTEM
TO WISHBONE TACTICAL TENDENCIES

In order to adjust our defense for sets, keys, and responsibilities we must take into consideration that they are trying to run the triple-options off of two of our defensive down linemen without blocking them on the line-of-scrimmage at the point-of-attack. We take a defensive attitude that there are no reasons to give them any options. We will simply force them to pitch very quickly, and make it a high risk play. We will force them to block our two defensive down linemen on the line of-scrimmage. If they don't, our defensive tackles, interior linebackers, and ends are going to hit their fullback regardless of who has the ball. A quick pitch will give our defense a chance for reaction and pursuit for outside containment. Defensive hesitation results in time needed for options, and offensive flanking advantages on the pitch-

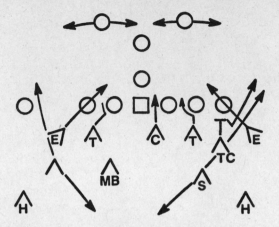

Figure 10-4
53 Call

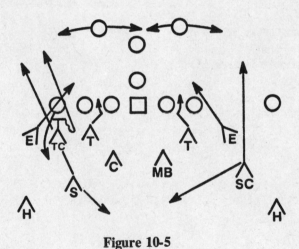

Figure 10-5
44 Call

outs. Our split cornerback and safety will apply invert zone rotation in their reactions to the outside. The interior linebacker to the split side will back up the split cornerback, and the safety will back up the tight cornerback in their outside containments. This can only be done by their reactions without hesitation, and forcing a quick pitchout.

We need to make some special adjustments in our defensive alignments, and maintain our basic techniques. Our tackle to the split side on a 53 call will shade the inside shoulder of the offensive tackle, and apply his basic reach technique on the over and off their split side guard. This gives us our basic split 44 alignment to the split side of our 53 defense. The tight side will make their basic 53 alignments. The defense will apply their split 44 alignments and techniques to both the split and tight sides on a 44 call. This should always put our tackle in control of the offensive tackle and guard gaps. Our tackle are responsible to hit the fullback on every play. The interior linebackers' first priority is to back up the tackles, and their second priority is to back up the ends. The ends hit the quarterback on every play that comes their way. The defensive secondary use zone coverage on both 44 and 53 calls.

FIGURES 10-4 and 10-5 show our set adjustments, keys, and responsibilities against the Wishbone with both 53 and 44 calls.

53 CALL (Figure 10-4) shows our split cornerback set in the triangle of the left split side reading and reacting to the halfback to his side. Our safety is set to the right reading and reacting to the halfback to his side. Our tight cornerback applies his basic bump and recovery technique on their right tight end. The middle linebacker keys the fullback and plays him inside into his defensive tackle before any outside pursuit. The combo shoots the gap between center and tight side guard.

44 CALL (Figure 10-5) shows our split cornerback set in the triangle of the right split side reading and reacting to the halfback to his side. Our safety is set to the left reading and reacting to the halfback to his side. Our tight cornerback applies his basic bump and recovery technique on their left tight end. The combo and middle linebacker keys the fullback and plays him inside into his defensive tackle before any outside pursuit.

INDIVIDUAL ADJUSTMENTS AGAINST
THE TRIPLE OPTION SEQUENCE

The individual sets, keys, responsibilities, techniques, and reactions are shown and explained for each position against the triple option sequences. The 53 calls will be applied to our left, and the 44 calls will be applied to our right as follows:

FIGURES 10-6 and 10-7 show the triple option sequences being run to our split sides.

53 Call vs. triple option to our left split side (Figure 10-6)

LEFT END:

1. SET-Outside and facing through their tackle.
2. KEY-Quarterback.
3. RESPONSIBILITIES-Inside shoulder to quarterback.

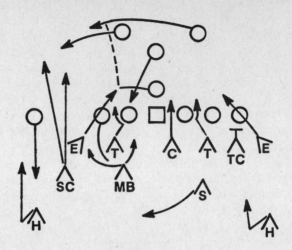

Fugure 10-6
53 Call

4. TECHNIQUE-Charge through the set of their tackle hitting the quarterback.

5. REACTION-Hit the quarterback, or force him to pitch before the halfback gets to a position flanking his offensive tackle.

RIGHT END:

1. SET-Outside and facing through their tight end.
2. KEY-Quarterback.
3. RESPONSIBILITIES-Inside shoulder to quarterback.
4. TECHNIQUE-Charge through the set of the right tight end to a position two yards behind the tackle.
5. REACTION-Trail the quarterback.

LEFT TACKLE:

1. SET-Shade inside shoulder of offensive tackle.
2. KEY-Fullback and ball.
3. RESPONSIBILITIES-Fullback, inside tackle gap.
4. TECHNIQUE-Forearm shiver reach on offensive guard.
5. REACTION-Hit fullback.

RIGHT TACKLE:

1. SET-Head up, on offensive tackle.

2. KEY-Fullback and ball.
3. RESPONSIBILITIES-Fullback, inside tackle gap.
4. TECHNIQUE-Forearm shiver control on offensive tackle.
5. REACTION-Inside tackle gap, pursuit.

COMBO: (NOSE MAN)

1. SET-Center and guard gap to right tight side.
2. KEY-Center's hands and ball.
3. RESPONSIBILITIES-The gap.
4. TECHNIQUE-Shoot the gap.
5. REACTION-Grab legs.

MIDDLE LINEBACKER:

1. SET-Over the left guard and off the L.O.S.
2. KEY-Reads left guard through to the fullback.
3. RESPONSIBILITIES-Fullback Outside pursuit.
4. TECHNIQUE-Play the football.
5. REACTION-Left.

SPLIT CORNERBACK:

1. SET-Triangle left split.
2. KEY-Reads near side halfback.
3. RESPONSIBILITIES-Outside containment, Baker rotation.
4. TECHNIQUE-Outside charge.
5. REACTION-Outside penetration for pitchout.

TIGHT CORNERBACK:

1. SET-To right side, head-up on tight end at L.O.S. in a low two point stance.
2. KEY-Tight end's movement, near side halfback.
3. RESPONSIBILITIES-Force tight end to his outside. Inside control with outside reaction.
4. TECHNIQUE-Bump and recovery.
5. REACTION-Easy zone coverage.

SAFETY

1. SET-6 to 8 yards off tight end to our right.
2. KEY-Read nearside halfback.
3. RESPONSIBILITIES-Right side pitchout, Baker rotation.

4. TECHNIQUE-Zone coverage.

5. REACTION-Rotate to Baker.

LEFT HALFBACK:

1. SET-10 to 12 yards off split end.

2. KEY-Read split end.

3. RESPONSIBILITIES-Charlie zone, outside containment.

4. TECHNIQUE-Zone coverage.

5. REACTION-Play split end to outside.

RIGHT HALFBACK:

1. SET-10 to 12 yards off tight end.

2. KEY-Read tight end.

3. RESPONSIBILITIES-Able zone, outside containment.

4. TECHNIQUE-Zone coverage.

5. REACTION-Stay home.

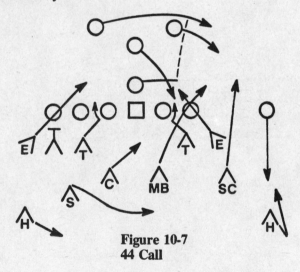

Figure 10-7
44 Call

44 Call vs. triple option to our right split side (Figure 10-7)

LEFT END:

1. SET-Outside, facing through tight end.

2. KEY-Quarterback.

3. RESPONSIBILITIES-Inside shoulder to quarterback.

4. TECHNIQUE-Charge through set of their tight end to a position two yards behind the offensive tackle.

5. REACTION-Trail the quarterback.

RIGHT END:

1. SET-Outside, facing through the offensive tackle.
2. KEY-Quarterback.
3. RESPONSIBILITIES-Inside shoulder to quarterback.
4. TECHNIQUE-Charge through the set of their tight end, hitting the quarterback.
5. REACTION-Hit the quarterback, or force him to pitch before the halfback gets to a position flanking his offensive tackle.

TACKLES: (BOTH LEFT AND RIGHT)

1. SETS-Shade inside shoulders of their tackles.
2. KEYS-Fullback and ball.
3. RESPONSIBILITIES-Fullback, inside tackle gap.
4. TECHNIQUES-Forearm shiver reach on offensive guards.
5. REACTIONS-Hit fullback.

COMBO: (LEFT INTERIOR LINEBACKER)

1. SET-Over the left guard and off the L.O.S.
2. KEY-Read left guard through to the fullback.
3. RESPONSIBILITIES-Fullback, lateral pursuit.
4. TECHNIQUE-Play the football.
5. REACTION-Right, stop fullback cutback.

MIDDLE LINEBACKER: (RIGHT INTERIOR)

1. SET-Over the right guard and off the L.O.S.
2. KEY-Read right guard through to the fullback.
3. RESPONSIBILITIES-Fullback-outside pursuit.
4. TECHNIQUE-Play the football.
5. REACTION-Right.

SPLIT CORNERBACK:

1. SET-Triangles right split.
2. KEY-Read near side halfback.
3. RESPONSIBILITIES-Outside containment.

4. TECHNIQUE-Outside charge.

5. REACTION-Outside penetration for pitchout.

TIGHT CORNERBACK:

1. SET-To left side, head-up on tight end at L.O.S. in a low two point stance.
2. KEY-Tight end's movement, near side halfback.
3. RESPONSIBILITIES-Force tight end to his outside. Inside control with outside reaction.
4. TECHNIQUE-Bump and recovery.
5. REACTION-Dog zone coverage.

SAFETY:

1. SET-6 to 8 yard off tight end to our left.
2. KEY-Read nearside halfback.
3. RESPONSIBILITIES-Left side pitchout, Baker rotation.
4. TECHNIQUE-Zone coverage.
5. REACTION-Rotate to Baker.

HALFBACKS (LEFT AND RIGHT)

1. SETS-10 to 12 yards off respective tight and split ends.
2. KEYS-Read respective tight and split ends.
3. RESPONSIBILITIES-Charlie and Able zones respectively.
4. TECHNIQUES-Zone coverage.
5. REACTIONS-Right

FIGURES 10-8 and 10-9 show the triple option sequences being run against a 53 defense to our left tight side, and a 44 defense to our right tight side. There are variations for each position in sets, keys, responsibilities, and techniques from running the triple option sequence to the split side. (Figures 10-6 and 10-7).

53 Call vs. triple option to our left tight side (Figure 10-8)

LEFT END:

1. SET-Outside and facing through the tight end.
2. KEY-Quarterback.
3. RESPONSIBILITIES-Inside shoulder to quarterback.
4. TECHNIQUE-Charge through the set of their tight end hitting the quarterback.

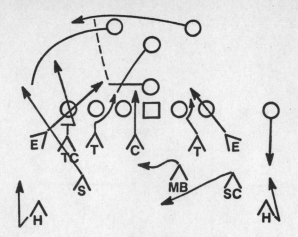

Figure 10-8
53 Call

5. REACTION-Hit the quarterback, or force him to pitch fast before the halfback gets to a position flanking his offensive tackle.

RIGHT END:

1. SET-Outside and facing through the tackle.
2. KEY-Quarterback.
3. RESPONSIBILITIES-Inside shoulder to quarterback.
4. TECHNIQUE-Charge through the set of the left tackle to a position two yards behind him.
5. REACTION-Trail the quarterback.

LEFT TACKLE:

1. SET-Head on defensive tackle.
2. KEY-Fullback and ball.
3. RESPONSIBILITIES-Fullback, inside tackle gap.
4. TECHNIQUE-Forearm shiver control on offensive tackle.
5. REACTION-Hit fullback.

RIGHT TACKLE:

1. SET-Shade inside shoulder of offensive tackle.
2. KEY-Fullback and ball.
3. RESPONSIBILITIES-Fullback inside tackle gap.

4. TECHNIQUE-Forearm shiver reach on offensive guard.
5. REACTION-Inside tackle gap, pursuit.

COMBO: (NOSE MAN)

1. SET-Center and left guard gap to tight side.
2. KEY-Center's hands and ball.
3. RESPONSIBILITIES-The gap.
4. TECHNIQUE-Shoot the gap.
5. REACTION-Grab legs.

MIDDLE LINEBACKER:

1. SET-Over the right guard and off the L.O.S.
2. KEY-Read right guard through to the fullback.
3. RESPONSIBILITIES-Fullback, pursuit.
4. TECHNIQUE-Play the football.
5. REACTION-Right pursuit.

SPLIT CORNERBACK:

1. SET-Triangles right split.
2. KEY-Rear near side halfback.
3. RESPONSIBILITIES-Outside containment, Baker rotation.
4. TECHNIQUE-Zone coverage.
5. REACTION-Baker rotation.

TIGHT CORNERBACK:

1. SET-To left side, head-up on tight end at L.O.S. in a low two point stance.
2. KEY-Tight end's movement, near side halfback.
3. RESPONSIBILITIES-Force tight end to outside. Inside control with outside reaction.
4. TECHNIQUE-Bump and recovery.
5. REACTION-Penetrate for pitchout.

SAFETY:

1. SET-6 to 8 yards off tight end to our left.
2. KEY-Read near side halfback.
3. RESPONSIBILITIES-Left side pitchout, Baker rotation.
4. TECHNIQUE-Outside charge.
5. REACTION-Outside penetration for pitchout.

HALFBACKS: (LEFT AND RIGHT)

1. SETS-10 to 12 yards off respective tight and split ends.
2. KEY-Read respective tight and split ends.
3. RESPONSIBILITIES-Charlie and Able zones respectively.
4. TECHNIQUE-Zone coverage.
5. REACTION-Left.

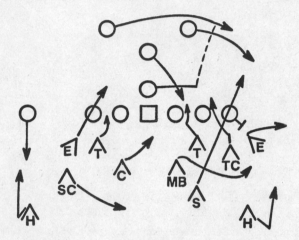

Figure 10-9
44 Call

44 Call vs. triple option to our right tight side (Figure 10-9)

LEFT END:

1. SET-Outside, facing through the offensive tackle.
2. KEY-Quarterback.
3. RESPONSIBILITIES-Inside shoulder to quarterback.
4. TECHNIQUE-Charge through the set of the offensive tackle to a position two yards behind them.
5. REACTION: Trail the quarterback.

RIGHT END:

1. SET-Outside facing through the tight end.
2. KEY-Quarterback.
3. RESPONSIBILITIES-When the tight end blocks out on him he takes an outside lateral pursuit to string out the pitchout.

4. TECHNIQUE-Immediate pursuit after contact.
5. REACTION-Right lateral pursuit.

TACKLES: (BOTH LEFT AND RIGHT)

1. SETS-Shade inside shoulders of tackles.
2. KEYS-Quarterback.
3. RESPONSIBILITIES-Fullback, inside tackle gap.
4. TECHNIQUES-Forearm shiver reach on offensive guards.
5. REACTIONS-Hit fullback.

COMBO: (LEFT INTERIOR LINEBACKER)

1. SET-Over the left guard and off the L.O.S.
2. KEY-Read left guard through to the fullback.
3. RESPONSIBILITIES-Fullback, lateral pursuit.
4. TECHNIQUE-Play the football.
5. REACTION-Right, stop fullback cut back.

MIDDLE LINEBACKER: (RIGHT INTERIOR)

1. SET-Over the right guard and off the L.O.S.
2. KEY-Read right guard through to the fullback.
3. RESPONSIBILITIES-Fullback, outside pursuit.
4. TECHNIQUE-Play the football.
5. REACTION-Right.

SPLIT CORNERBACK:

1. SET-Triangles left split.
2. KEY-Read nearside halfback.
3. RESPONSIBILITIES-Outside containment, Baker rotation.
4. TECHNIQUE-Zone coverage.
5. REACTION-Rotate to Baker.

TIGHT CORNERBACK:

1. SET-To right side on tight end at L.O.S. in a low two point stance.
2. KEY-Tight end's movement, nearside halfback.
3. RESPONSIBILITIES-When the tight end blocks out on defensive end, he penetrates the L.O.S. forcing the quarterback to pitch.
4. TECHNIQUE-Bump and recovery.
5. REACTION-Hit the quarterback.

SAFETY:

1. SET-6 to 8 yards off tight end to our right.
2. KEY-Read nearside halfback.
3. RESPONSIBILITIES-Right side pitchout, Baker rotation.
4. TECHNIQUE-Outside charge.
5. REACTION-Right penetration.

HALFBACKS: (LEFT AND RIGHT)

1. SETS-10 to 12 yards off respective split and tight ends.
2. KEYS-Read respective split and tight ends.
3. RESPONSIBILITIES-Charlie and Able zones respectively.
4. TECHNIQUES-Zone coverage.
5. REACTIONS-Right.

This completes the adjustments of both 53 and 44 defense against the triple option sequences from the Wishbone. Next we will show the adjustments against the Wishbone passing attack.

SECONDARY ADJUSTMENTS AGAINST
THE WISHBONE PASSING GAME

Most Wishbone systems use playaction passes with a fake to the fullback or the halfback option passes. The halfback option passes put the most pressure on our outside containment. We use zone coverage with invert safety and split cornerback rotation. Both cornerbacks must force the halfbacks on their option passes. The interior linebackers and safety must cover the hook areas and flats. The halfbacks maintain their zone coverage.

Our ends and tackles apply their basic containments and pass rush. The sets, keys, responsibilities, techniques, and reactions of each position of our pass defenders will be covered. These positions are: The two halfbacks, safety, split cornerback, tight cornerback, combo, and middle linebacker.

FIGURES 10-10 and 10-11 show Wishbone fullback playaction passes being run to the left against our 53 defense, and being run to the right against our 44 defense.

53 Call vs. wishbone playaction pass to our left (Figure 10-10)

HALFBACKS: (BOTH LEFT AND RIGHT)

1. SETS-10 to 12 yards, outside deep zones.
2. KEYS-Outside receivers (Split and tight ends)
3. RESPONSIBILITIES-Charlie and Able zones respectively.

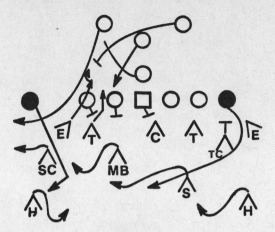

Figure 10-10
53 Call

4. TECHNIQUES-Zone coverage.

5. REACTION-Deep receivers in their zones.

SAFETY:

1. SET- 6 to 8 yards off their tight end to our right.

2. KEY-Read their near side halfback.

3. RESPONSIBILITIES-Nearside halfback Easy zone, Baker rotation.

4. TECHNIQUE-Zone coverage.

5. REACTION-Rotate to Baker.

SPLIT CORNERBACK:

1. SET-Triangles left split.

2. KEY-Read their nearside halfback.

3. RESPONSIBILITIES-Nearside halfback to Dog, Baker rotation.

4. TECHNIQUE-Zone coverage.

5. REACTION-Pick up the near halfback in the flat Dog zone.

TIGHT CORNERBACK:

1. SET-On right tight end in a low two point stance.

2. KEY-Tight end's movement.

3. RESPONSIBILITIES-Force halfback pass option, cover Easy.

4. TECHNIQUE-Bump and recovery.

5. REACTION-Covers Easy zone.

MIDDLE LINEBACKER:

1. SET-Over their left guard and off the L.O.S.
2. KEY-Reads left guard through to the fullback.
3. RESPONSIBILITIES-Left hook through to Dog flat.
4. TECHNIQUE-Zone coverage.
5. REACTION-Left hook area, back up split cornerback.

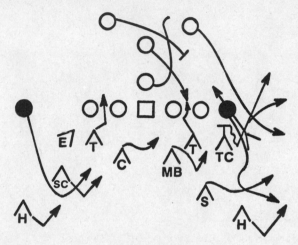

Figure 10-11
44 Call

44 Call vs. wishbone playaction pass to our right (Figure 10-11)

HALFBACKS: (BOTH LEFT AND RIGHT)

Same as with 53 call.

SAFETY:

1. SET-6 to 8 yards off their tight end to our right.
2. KEY-Read their nearside halfback.
3. RESPONSIBILITIES-Nearside halfback Easy zone.
4. TECHNIQUE-Zone coverage.
5. REACTION-Pick up their nearside halfback in Easy zone.

SPLIT CORNERBACKER:

1. SET-Triangles left split.
2. KEY-Read their nearside halfback.

3. RESPONSIBILITIES-Nearside halfback to Dog, Baker rotation.
4. TECHNIQUE-Zone coverage.
5. REACTION Baker rotation.

TIGHT CORNERBACK:

1. SET-On right tight end in a low two point stance.
2. KEY-Tight end's movement.
3. RESPONSIBILITIES-Cover Easy.
4. TECHNIQUE-Bump and recovery.
5. REACTION-Pick up nearside halfback in Easy flat.

INTERIOR LINEBACKERS (BOTH COMBO AND MIDDLE LINEBACKER)

1. SETS-Over respective offensive guards off the LO.OS.
2. KEYS-Read guard through to the fullback.
3. RESPONSIBILITIES-Hook areas.
4. TECHNIQUES-Zone coverage.
5. REACTIONS-Right back up, right hook respectively.

FIGURES 10-12 and 10-13 show Wishbone halfback option passes being run to the left against our 53 defense, and being run to the right against our 44 defense. Their halfbacks can put additional pressure on our outside containment with pass and run options. Our cornerbacks will force the pass with backup coverage from our safety and interior linebackers.

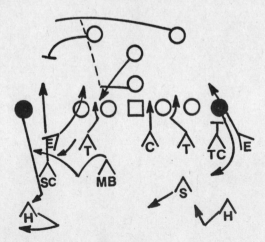

Figure 10-12
53 Call

53 Call vs. wishbone halfback option pass to our left (Figure 10-12)

HALFBACKS: (BOTH LEFT AND RIGHT)

Basically the same as Figures 10-10 and 10-11.

SAFETY:

1. SET-6 to 8 yards off their tight end to our right.
2. KEY-Read their near side halfback.
3. RESPONSIBILITIES-Nearside halfback Easy zone, Baker rotation.
4. TECHNIQUE-Zone coverage.
5. REACTION-Rotation to Baker.

SPLIT CORNERBACK:

1. SET-Triangle left split.
2. KEY-Read their nearside halfback.
3. RESPONSIBILITIES-Force halfback to pass, Baker rotation.
4. TECHNIQUE-Zone coverage.
5. REACTION-Penetrate outside to force halfback to pass.

TIGHT CORNERBACK:

1. SET-On right tight end in a low two point stance.
2. KEY-Tight end's movement.
3. RESPONSIBILITIES-Force tight end to outside, Easy zone.
4. TECHNIQUE-Bump and recovery.
5. REACTION-Covers Easy zone.

MIDDLE LINEBACKER:

1. SET-Over their left guard and off the L.O.S.
2. KEY-Reads left guard through to the fullback.
3. RESPONSIBILITIES-Left hook through to Dog flat.
4. TECHNIQUE-Zone coverage.
5. REACTION-Left hook, Dog flat.

44 Call vs. wishbone halfback option pass to our right (Figure 10-13)

HALFBACK: (BOTH LEFT AND RIGHT)

Basically the same as Figures 10-10 and 10-11.

SAFETY:

1. SET-6 to 8 yards off their tight end to our right.

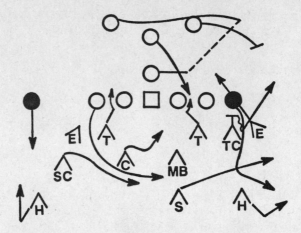

Figure 10-13
44 Call

2. KEY-Read their nearside halfback.
3. RESPONSIBILITIES-Near halfback Easy zone, Baker rotation.
4. TECHNIQUE-Zone coverage.
5. REACTION-Pick up tight end in Easy zone.

SPLIT CORNERBACK:

1. SET-Triangle left split.
2. KEY-Read their nearside halfback.
3. RESPONSIBILITIES-Force halfback to pass, Baker rotation.
4. TECHNIQUE-Zone coverage.
5. REACTION-Rotate to Baker.

TIGHT CORNERBACK:

1. SET-On right tight end in low two point stance.
2. KEY-Tight end's movement.
3. RESPONSIBILITIES-Force tight end to outside, force halfback to pass.
4. TECHNIQUE-Bump and recovery.
5. REACTION-Rush halfback on pitch.

INTERIOR LINEBACKERS: (COMBO AND MIDDLE LINEBACKER)

1. SETS-Over their respective guards, and off the L.O.S.

2. KEYS-Read their respective guards through to the fullback.
3. RESPONSIBILITIES-Hook areas through to the flats.
4. TECHNIQUES-Zone coverage.
5. REACTIONS-Right respective back up, hook area.

Though the Wishbone formation has a passing disadvantage in its basic alignment, we cannot afford to ignore it. Any team that has the balance of personnel to run the triple option from a Wishbone formation has the ability to pass from the disadvantages of the alignment. Usually, a well schooled Wishbone quarterback does not have the background to pick your pass defense to pieces. This does not mean he does not have the ability, but that he has not had the experience with their offensive approach. If you ever run into a halfback that can naturally pick a defense apart on a pass run option, there will be no defense against the Wishbone. This is natural ability that is not coached. I have never seen or heard of a halfback who could naturally do this consistently. There are quarterbacks who might. This has led to the current, popular veer offense.

We take the same defensive attitude as the pros. If the offense values the longevity of their quarterback, they had better not run the option against us. If the offense does not feel their fullback can run over our two defensive tackles head-on, then they had better block them on every play. Otherwise, their quarterback and fullback will be hit on every play.

I realize that high schools do not have nearly as much time and money invested in their quarterbacks as the pros, but it is still the key offensive position. We basically use the options. There is one team on our schedule for which we always totally eliminate our options because of measures to protect our quarterback from the backside, and use our tight end to block him to the frontside. We would never allow ourselves to be dependent on the option because our quarterback is very important to us.

11

STOPPING THE VEER WITH THE COMBO SYSTEM

APPLYING THE COMBO SYSTEM
VS. THE VEER OFFENSE

The veer-offense is a result of integrating the triple option techniques into a pro-set alignment to increase the passing potential. The split backfield set behind pro-set lines with a wide flanker and split end presents a better tactical balance for running and passing than that of the Wishbone formations. The inside and outside halfback dives replace the fullback bellies as the first phase of the triple option sequences. The same backfield approaches and blocking theories are applied. The advantages are the integration of Winged T techniques and an increasing threat of passing. The disadvantages are the elimination of the lead blocker out of the backfield, and a higher risk of fumbles at the line of scrimmage. Though the basic concepts are easy to understand, the veer requires even more time in perfecting the techniques than the time consuming teaching processes of the Wishbone.

CHARACTERISTICS OF THE VEER OFFENSE

Both the Wishbone and Veer are similiar in their basic concepts, with their major threats being to the outside. The difference is that one is a three-back offense, and the other is a two back offense. The Veer offenses do not have a lead back in their outside options, unless they eliminate the fake of the first option. The veer has sacrificed the lead back for a better passing formation. Our defensive alignments against the pro-set put our players in a much better pre-snap position for outside containment than what we had against the Wishbone. Inside and outside halfback dives are the first options with the Veer. Our defensive alignments usually force the inside Veers to our tight side and the outside veers to our split side. The same basic blocking schemes of releasing offensive linemen at the points-of-attacks are applied as was with the Wishbone.

FIGURE 11-1 shows the basic Veer formations with split backfields.

The first two diagrams show the pro-sets to the left (top) and the right (top). These are the two most common formations used with the Veer sequence, and what we will adjust our defenses against. The wide flanker and tight end are the two receivers to the frontside of the formations, and the split end is the receiver to the backside.

The second two diagrams show the slot sets to the left (bottom) and the right (bottom). The same defensive set adjustments against these front alignments have already been covered in Chapter 9.

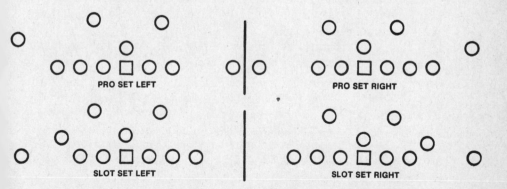

Figure 11-1
Basic Veer Series

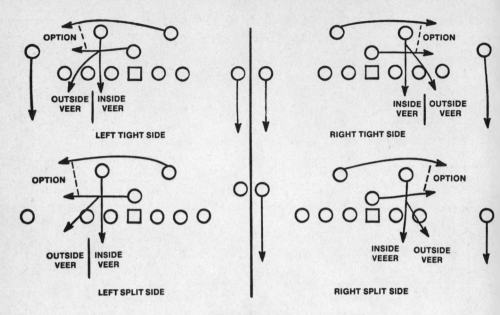

**Figure 11-2
Basic Veer Series**

FIGURE 11-2 shows the triple option sequences run to both the left and right frontsides and backsides. There are both inside and outside hand-offs in all the basic sequences. These halfback dives are the first options of the sequence. Many of these hand-offs are predetermined, and in reality are not options. This is because many quarterbacks cannot read it, and this is especially true at the high school levels. It is difficult for an outsider to tell if their first options are phoney or real.

Their left frontside series is run to our left tight side. The first play of the sequence is usually the inside veer. The wide flanker is the lead blocker for the outside options. (top, left diagram)

Their right frontside series is run to our right tight side. The first play of the sequence is usually the inside veer. The wide flanker is the lead blocker for the outside options. (top, right diagram)

Their left backside series is run to our left split side. The first play of the sequence is usually the outside veer. Their split end is the lead blocker for the outside options. (bottom, left diagram)

Their right backside series is run to our right split side. The first play of the sequence is usually the outside veer. Their split end is the lead blocker for the outside options. (bottom, right diagram)

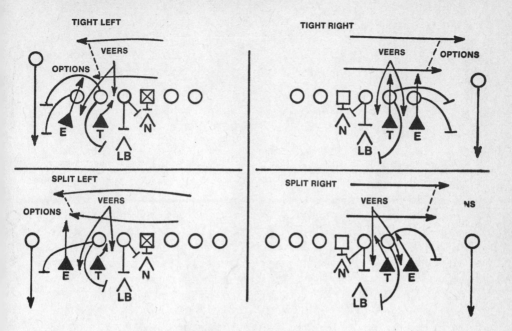

Figure 11-3
Veer Blocking System

FIGURE 11-3 shows the basic blocking system used with the Veer offense. The only differences from the Wishbone are the adjustments to the backfield patterns, since the Veer hand offs are faster without the angle of the fullback's set.

The tight left side of the Veer shows the blocking for their frontside sequence to our left. Their offensive tackle blocks the inside linebacker on inside veers, and pulls as a lead blocker on the wide option, while the tight end blocks the cornerback. Their offensive tackle blocks the defensive tackle on both the outside veer and option, while the tight end pulls as a lead blocker on the wide option. (top, left panel)

The tight right side of the veer shows the blocking for their frontside sequences to our right. This is the same as it was to our left. (top, right panel)

The split left side of the veer shows the blocking for their backside sequence to our left. Since there is no tight end to that side, their tackle releases on linebackers on inside veers, blocks the tackle on outside veers, and pulls as a lead blocker on all wide options. (bottom, left panel)

The split right side of the veer shows the blocking for their backside blocking to our right. This is the same as it was to our left. (Bottom, right panel)

Keep in mind that there are many variations to the basic blocking scheme, and it is based on the same principles as was used with the Wishbone.

ADJUSTING THE COMBO SYSTEM
TO VEER TACTICAL TENDENCIES

As strange as it might seem, it is easier for us to adjust our alignments to the veer than it is the Wishbone. This is because our basic adjustments put us in natural presnap-positions for outside containment, we do not have to worry about the lead back out of the backfield, and we are in good position to protect against the pass. With the Wishbone we had to make special adjustments against outside containment of their running game dependent on the abilities of their personnel to put the ball in the air. With the veer we have no special tactical adjustments to make. These reversed tactical tendencies of our combo defensive system should make any coach study it with much interest. If the Wishbone offense has the personnel, it could be one of the two greatest tactical offenses in football. Because of the time in which they have to teach the techniques, they are tactically limited to the personnel from which they have to work. If they have great personnel, it doesn't make much difference what they run. It would be easier to prepare a defense against a Wishbone than it would against the Princeton bucklateral series from the unbalanced single wing. We all know that Oklahoma has better personnel than Princeton did in the late 40's, and early 50's. Can some of you college coaches imagine preparing your defense against Oklahoma running the Bucklateral series, instead of the Wishbone? Don't worry!! The triple option is easier to teach, and the coach might survive a loss or two with the Wishbone. If he had a loss or two with horse-and-buggy football, he would probably be fired. If I were at your level, I would only have the courage to do what you do. I am not too sure that there is not one coach that is about to let his tactical heart overrule his tactical head. If he does, it is not because "Necessity is the mother of invention." It will be because consistent success has left him one last challenge. This could make him the greatest football innovator of all times. It would be nice to see a tactical innovator come from the pro-ranks with influences on the lower levels, instead of from the college level.

Many coaches are copy-cats, because they stick to the security of what has proven to be tactically successful. They are too busy with survival or self-egos to be innovative. The professional coach worries about personnel and the drafts, the college coach worries about recruitment and tactics, and the high school coach worries about tactics and what he has to work with. The difference has been in the levels of personnel with a large gap in tactical innovations. The innovations very often come from the lower levels because of less personnel and pressure. The veer offense is closing the tactical gap between the college and pro-levels, and the high schools will naturally take care of themselves. We might even see the day when a pro-coach can talk to high school coaches without using a college coach as an interpreter. The only reason a pro coach doesn't have the time to talk tactics to high school coaches, is because he knows that they do not have the concept of the talented personnel that he is working with. How could they, when they probably have not been one themselves. The veer offenses are college techniques applied to pro formations. Pro tactics are finally beginning to have some influences on the lower levels. The pro concept of defense makes more sense to us at a high school level, than what has generally been accepted at the college level.

Again we will eliminate the options by forcing the pitch, or force them to block our two down defensive linemen on the line-of-scrimmage at the point-of-attacks. Our defensive front will apply their basic sets, keys, and responsibilities on both 53 and 44 calls. Our pass defenders apply zone coverage with invert rotation of the safety and split cornerback. The safety and split cornerback read the near running back through to the other back, and react to their patterns. The interior linebackers read the ball through the running backs on their reaction. We like to switch to man-to-man coverage on short yardage or running situations. The safety covers the tight end, and both cornerbacks pick up the first man out of their backfield. The safety and tight cornerback are responsible for outside containment of the triple-options to the tightside, and the split corner and interior linebacker have the same responsibilities to the tight side.

FIGURES 11-4 and 11-5 show our set adjustments, keys, and responsibilities against the veer with both 53 and 44 calls.

53 CALL (Figure 11-4) shows our split cornerback set in the triangle of the right split to their backside. He reads the backside halfback through to their frontside halfback, and reacts to their patterns. Our safety sets to the left and reads and reacts to the tight end (man-to-man coverage), or their patterns of the running backs (zone coverage). Our tight cornerback applies his bump and recovery techniques on their tight end to the left, before reacting to the running backs' patterns. The middle linebacker plays the dives before he backs-up the wide options. The ends, tackles, combo, and halfbacks use their basic set adjustment, techniques, and responsibilities for a 53 call.

44 CALL (Figure 11-5) shows our split cornerback set in the triangle of the left split to their backside. He reads the backside halfback through to their frontside halfback, and reacts to their patterns. Our safety sets to the right and reads and reacts to the tight end (man-to-man coverage), or the patterns of

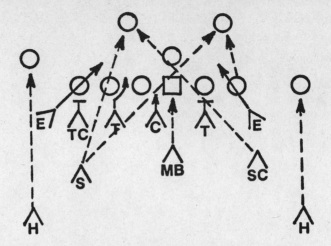

Figure 11-4
53 Call

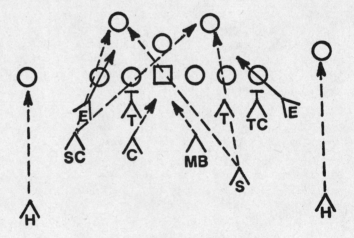

Figure 11-5
44 Call

their running backs (zone coverage). Our tight cornerback applies his bump and recovery techniques on their tight end right, before reacting to the running backs' patterns. The interior linebackers play the dives before they back up the outside options. The ends, tackles, and halfbacks use their basic set adjustments, technique and responsibilities for a 44 call.

INDIVIDUAL ADJUSTMENTS AGAINST THE VEER SEQUENCE

The individual sets, keys, responsibilities, techniques, and reactions are shown and explained for each position against the veer sequences. The 53 calls will be applied to the left, and the 44 calls will be applied to the right as follows:

FIGURES 11-6 and 11-7 show the triple option sequences being run to the front side of the veer offense.

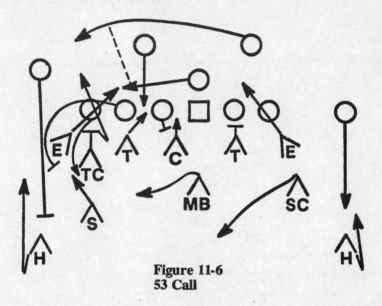

Figure 11-6
53 Call

53 Call vs. veer to our left tight side (Figure 11-6)

LEFT END:

1. SET-Outside, facing through their tight end.
2. KEY-Quarterback.
3. RESPONSIBILITIES-Inside shoulder to quarterback.
4. TECHNIQUE-Charge through the set of their tight end hitting the quarterback.
5. REACTION-Hit the quarterback, or force him to pitch before the halfback gets to a position flanking his offensive tackle.

RIGHT END:

1. SET-Outside, facing through their tackle

2. KEY-Quarterback.

3. RESPONSIBILITIES-Inside shoulder to the quarterback.

4. TECHNIQUE-Charge through the set of their tackle hitting the quarterback.

5. REACTION-Trail the quarterback.

LEFT TACKLE:

1. SET-Shade inside shoulder of offensive tackle.

2. KEY-Near halfback and ball.

3. RESPONSIBILITIES-Veer hand-off, inside tackle gap.

4. TECHNIQUE-Forearm shiver on offensive tackle.

5. REACTION-Hit the near halfback on hand off.

RIGHT TACKLE:

1. SET-Head up, on their offensive guard.

2. KEY-Near halfback and ball.

3. RESPONSIBILITIES-Veer hand off and pursuit.

4. TECHNIQUE-Forearm shiver, read the head.

5. REACTION-Left pursuit.

COMBO: (NOSE MAN)

1. SET-Center, and guard gap to left tight side.

2. KEY-Center's hands and ball.

3. RESPONSIBILITIES-The gap.

4. TECHNIQUE-Shoot the gap.

5. REACTION-Grab legs.

MIDDLE LINEBACKER:

1. SET-Over the center, and off the L.O.S.

2. KEY-Reads the backfield pattern.

3. RESPONSIBILITIES-Veer hand-off outside pursuit.

4. TECHNIQUE-Play the football.

5. REACTION-Left.

SPLIT CORNERBACK:

1. SET-Triangles right split.

2. KEY-Reads nearside halfback.

3. RESPONSIBILITIES-Outside containment, Baker rotation
4. TECHNIQUE-Outside charge.
5. REACTION-Rotate to Baker.

TIGHT CORNERBACK:

1. SET-To left side, head-up on tight end at L.O.S.
2. KEY-Tight end's movement, nearside halfback.
3. RESPONSIBILITIES-Force tight end to his outside. Inside control with outside reaction.
4. TECHNIQUE-Bump and recovery.
5. REACTION-Inside penetration on pitchout.

SAFETY:

1. SET-6 to 8 yards off tight end to our left.
2. KEY-Read tight end through to back's pattern.
3. RESPONSIBILITIES-Left side pitchout, Baker rotation.
4. TECHNIQUE-Zone coverage.
5. REACTION-Left penetration for pitchout.

LEFT HALFBACK:

1. SET-10 to 12 yards off wide flanker.
2. KEY-Read wide flanker.
3. RESPONSIBILITIES-Charlie zone, outside containment.
4. TECHNIQUE-Zone coverage.
5. REACTION-Play wide flanker to outside.

RIGHT HALFBACK:

1. SET-10 to 12 yards off split end.
2. KEY-Read split end.
3. RESPONSIBILITIES-Able zone, outside containment.
4. TECHNIQUE-Zone coverage.
5. REACTION-Stay home.

44 Call vs. veer to our right tight side (Figure 11-7)

LEFT END:

1. SET-Outside, facing through their tackle.

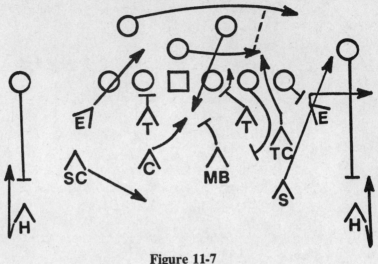

Figure 11-7
44 Call

2. KEY-Quarterback.

3. RESPONSIBILITIES-Inside shoulder to the quarterback.

4. TECHNIQUE-Charge through the set of their tackle, hitting the quarterback.

5. REACTION-Trail the quarterback.

RIGHT END:

1. SET-Outside, facing through their tight end.

2. KEY-Quarterback.

3. RESPONSIBILITIES-When tight end blocks out on him, outside lateral containment.

4. TECHNIQUE-Hit end, controlled recovery.

5. REACTION-Lateral pursuit right with pitchout.

LEFT TACKLE:

1. SET-Head-up, on their offensive guard.

2. KEY-Near halfback, and ball.

3. RESPONSIBILITIES-Veer hand off.

4. TECHNIQUE-Forearm shiver control, read the head.

5. REACTION-Fight pressure to right and pursue.

RIGHT TACKLE:

1. SET-Shade inside shoulder of their tackle.
2. KEY-Near halfback and ball.
3. RESPONSIBILITIES-Near halfback veer hand-off, inside tackle gap.
4. TECHNIQUE-Forearm shiver control on offensive tackle..
5. REACTION-Hit nearside halfback.

Combo: (left interior linebacker)

1. SET-Stack left defensive tackle.
2. KEY-Read near halfback and ball.
3. RESPONSIBILITIES-Veer hand-off, pursuit.
4. TECHNIQUE-Play the football.
5. REACTION-Back-up middle linebacker to right.

Middle linebacker:

1. SET-Right over their offensive guard and off the L.O.S.
2. KEY-Read the near halfback and ball.
3. RESPONSIBILITIES-Veer hand-off, pursuit.
4. TECHNIQUE-Play the football.
5. REACTION-Hand off, then pursuit right.

Split cornerback:

1. SET-Triangle left split.
2. KEY-Nearside halfback.
3. RESPONSIBILITIES-Outside containment, Baker rotation.
4. TECHNIQUE-Outside charge.
5. REACTION-Rotate to Baker.

Tight cornerback:

1. SET-To right side, head-up on tight end at L.O.S.
2. KEY-Tight end's movement, near side halfback.
3. RESPONSIBILITIES-Force tight end to his outside. Inside control. Soon as tight end blocks out on defensive end penetrate on quarterback.
4. TECHNIQUE-Charge.
5. REACTION-Hit the quarterback or force a quick pitch.

SAFETY:

1. SET-6 to 8 yards off tight end to our right.
2. KEY-Read tight end through to back's pattern.
3. RESPONSIBILITIES-Right side pitchout, Baker rotation.
4. TECHNIQUE-Zone coverage.
5. REACTION-Outside penetration for pitchout.

HALF BACKS: (BOTH LEFT AND RIGHT)

Zone: Sets, keys, responsibilities, and techniques for Charlie and Able respectively, and same as a 53 call. The reaction is to the right.

FIGURES 11-8 and 11-9 show the triple option sequences being run to the back side of the veer offense.

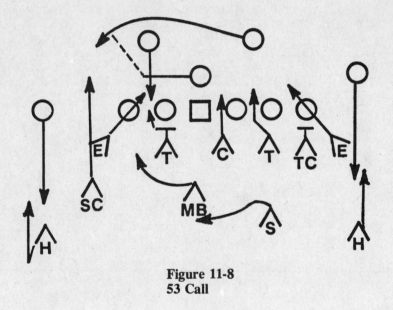

Figure 11-8
53 Call

44 Call vs. veer to our left split side (Figure 11-8)

LEFT END:

1. SET-Outside, facing through their tackle.
2. KEY-Quarterback.
3. RESPONSIBILITIES-Inside shoulder to quarterback.
4. TECHNIQUE-Charge through the set of their tackle hitting the quarterback.

5. REACTION-Hit the quarterback, or force him to pitch before the halfback gets to a possition flanking his offensive tackle.

RIGHT END:

1. SET-Outside, facing through their tight end.
2. KEY-Quarterback.
3. RESPONSIBILITIES-Inside shoulder to the quarterback.
4. TECHNIQUE-Charge through the set of their tight end hitting the quarterback.
5. REACTION-Trail the quarterback.

LEFT TACKLE:

1. SET-Head-up, on their offensive guard.
2. KEY-Near halfback and ball.
3. RESPONSIBILITIES-Veer hand-off and pursuit.
4. TECHNIQUE-Forearm shiver, read the head.
5. REACTION-Hit the near halfback on hand-off.

RIGHT TACKLE:

1. SET-Shape inside shoulder of offensive tackle.
2. KEY-Near halfback and ball.
3. RESPONSIBILITIES-Veer hand-off, inside tackle gap.
4. TECHNIQUE-Forearm shiver on offensive tackle.
5. REACTION-Left pursuit.

COMBO: (NOSE MAN)

1. SET-Center, and guard gap to right tight side.
2. KEY-Center's hands and ball.
3. RESPONSIBILITIES-The gap.
4. TECHNIQUE-Shoot the gap.
5. REACTION-Grab legs.

MIDDLE LINEBACKER:

1. SET-Over the center, and off the L.O.S.
2. KEY-Reads the backfield pattern.
3. RESPONSIBILITIES-Veer hand off, outside pursuit.
4. TECHNIQUE-Play the football.
5. REACTION-Left.

SPLIT CORNERBACK:

1. SET-Triangles left split.
2. KEY-Reads nearside halfback.
3. RESPONSIBILITIES-Outside containment, Baker rotation.
4. TECHNIQUE-Outside charge.
5. REACTION-Left penetration for pitchout.

TIGHT CORNERBACK:

1. SET-To right side, head-up on tight end at L.O.S.
2. KEY-Tight end's movement, nearside halfback.
3. RESPONSIBILITIES-Force tight end to his outside, Inside control with outside reaction.
4. TECHNIQUE-Bump and recovery.
5. REACTION-Easy coverage.

SAFETY:

1. SET-6 to 8 yard off tight end to our right.
2. KEY-Read tight end through to the back's pattern.
3. RESPONSIBILITIES-Right side pitchout, Baker rotation.
4. TECHNIQUE-Zone coverage.
5. REACTION-Baker rotation.

HALFBACKS: (BOTH LEFT AND RIGHT)

Zone: Sets, keys, responsibilities, and techniques for Charlie and Able respectively. The reaction is to the left.

44 Call vs. veer to our right split side (Figure 11-9)

LEFT END:

1. SET-Outside, facing through their tight end.
2. KEY-Quarterback.
3. RESPONSIBILITIES-Inside shoulder to the quarterback.
4. TECHNIQUE-Charge through the set of their tight end, hitting the quarterback.
5. REACTION-Trail the quarterback.

RIGHT END:

1. SET-Outside, facing through their tackle.

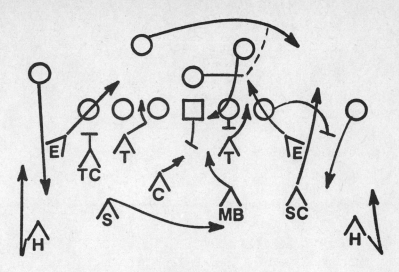

Figure 11-9
44 Call

2. KEY-Quarterback.
3. RESPONSIBILITIES-Inside shoulder to the quarterback.
4. TECHNIQUE-Charge through the set of the tackle hitting the quarterback.
5. REACTION-Hit the quarterback, or force him to pitch before the halfbacks gets to a position flanking his offensive tackle.

LEFT TACKLE:

1. SET-Shade inside shoulder of their tackle.
2. KEY-Near halfback and ball.
3. RESPONSIBILITIES-Near halfback and ball.
4. TECHNIQUE-Forearm shiver control on offensive tackle.
5. REACTION-Inside tackle gap, pursuit right.

RIGHT TACKLE:

1. SET-Head-up, on their offensive guard.
2. KEY-Near halfback and ball.
3. RESPONSIBILITIES-Near halfback veer hand-off outside guard gap.
4. TECHNIQUE-Forearm shiver control, read the heap.

5. REACTION-Fight pressure to the right.

COMBO: (LEFT INTERIOR LINEBACKER)

1. SET-Left over offensive guard, and off the L.O.S.
2. KEY-Read near halfback and ball.
3. RESPONSIBILITIES-Veer hand-off cut back.
4. TECHNIQUE-Play the football.
5. REACTION-Backup middle linebacker to the right.

MIDDLE LINEBACKER:

1. SET-Stack right defensive tackle.
2. KEY-Read near halfback and ball.
3. RESPONSIBILITIES-Inside veer hand-off, before pursuit to the right.
4. TECHNIQUE-Play the football.
5. REACTION-Inside hand-off, before pursuit to the right.

SPLIT CORNERBACK:

1. SET-Triangle right split.
2. KEY-Near halfback.
3. RESPONSIBILITIES-Outside containment, Baker rotation.
4. TECHNIQUE-Outside charge.
5. REACTION-Outside penetration for pitchout.

TIGHT CORNERBACK:

1. SET-To left tight side, head-up on tight end at L.O.S.
2. KEY-Tight end's movement, nearside halfback.
3. RESPONSIBILITIES-Force tight end to his outside, inside control, outside containment.
4. TECHNIQUE-Bump and recovery.
5. REACTION-Baker rotation.

HALFBACKS: (BOTH LEFT AND RIGHT)

Zone: Sets, keys, responsibilities, and techniques for Charlie and Able respectively, and same as a 53 call. The reaction is to the right.

This completes the adjustments of both the 53 and 44 defenses against the veer offenses for both the frontside and backside sequences. Next we will show the adjustments against the pro-sets from which the veer sequences are run.

SECONDARY ADJUSTMENTS AGAINST THE PRO-SETS

The pro set presents a natural formation from which to pass. Our combo defense is set in a natural position to handle the passing along with the outside containment of their veer triple option. We use zone coverage with invert safety and split cornerback rotation. Both cornerbacks must pick up the first back coming out of the backfield. The interior linebackers must cover the hook areas and backup the flats. The safety and halfbacks maintain their zone coverage.

Our ends and tackles apply their basic containments and pass rush. The sets, keys, responsibilities, techniques, and reactions of each position of our pass defenders will be covered. These positions are: the two halfbacks, safety, split cornerback, tight cornerback, combo, and middle linebacker.

FIGURES 11-10 and 11-11 show dropback passes from pro-sets being run to the left against our 53 defense, and being run to the right against our 44 defense.

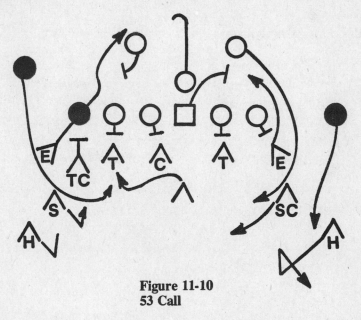

Figure 11-10
53 Call

53 Call vs. a dropback pass from a pro set to our left (Figure 11-10)

HALFBACKS: (BOTH LEFT AND RIGHT)

1. SETS-10 to 12 yards, outside deep zones.
2. KEYS-Outside receivers (wide flanker and split end)
3. RESPONSIBILITIES-Charlie and Able zones respectively.

4. TECHNIQUES-Zone coverage.

5. REACTIONS-Deep receivers in their zones.

SAFETY:

1. SET-6 to 8 yards off their tight end to our left.

2. KEY-Read their near halfback through their tight end.

3. RESPONSIBILITIES-Check Dog to Baker zone.

4. TECHNIQUE-Zone coverage.

5. REACTION-Check to wide receiver coming towards Baker zone.

SPLIT CORNERBACK:

1. SET-Triangle right split.

2. KEY-Read their near halfback.

3. RESPONSIBILITIES-Check Easy to Baker zone.

4. TECHNIQUE-Zone coverage.

5. REACTION-Pick up near halfback to Baker zone.

TIGHT CORNERBACK:

1. SET-On left tight end in a low two point stance.

2. KEY-Tight end's movement.

3. RESPONSIBILITIES-Cover Dog.

4. TECHNIQUE-Bump and recovery.

5. REACTION-Recover and cover the tight end in Dog zone.

MIDDLE LINEBACKER:

1. SET-Over the center, and off the L.O.S.

2. KEY-Reads the backfield pattern.

3. RESPONSIBILITIES-Veer hand-off, hook area to tight end side.

4. TECHNIQUE-Play football.

5. REACTION-Left hook area.

44 Call vs. a dropback pass from a pro-set to our right (Figure 11-11)

HALFBACKS: (BOTH LEFT AND RIGHT)

Same as with 53 call.

SAFETY:

1. SET-6 to 8 yards of their tight end to our right.

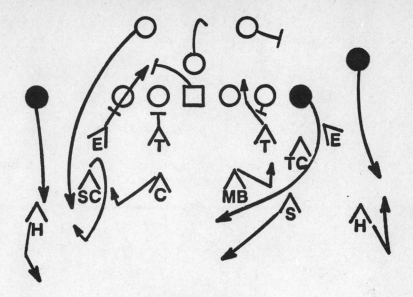

Figure 11-11
44 Call

2. KEY-Read near halfback through tight end.
3. RESPONSIBILITIES-Check Easy to Baker zone.
4. TECHNIQUE-Zone coverage.
5. REACTION-Pick up tight end in Baker zone.

SPLIT CORNERBACK:

1. SET-Triangles left split.
2. KEY-Read their nearside halfback.
3. RESPONSIBILITIES-Check Dog to Baker zone.
4. TECHNIQUE-Zone coverage.
5. REACTION-Pick up first back out of backfield.

TIGHT CORNERBACK:

1. SET-On right tight end in a low two point stance.
2. KEY-Tight end's movement.
3. RESPONSIBILITIES-Cover Easy.
4. TECHNIQUE-Bump and recovery.
5. REACTION-Easy flat.

INTERIOR LINEBACKERS: (BOTH COMBO AND MIDDLE LINEBACKER)

1. SETS-Over respective offensive guard off the L.O.S.
2. KEYS-Read near halfbacks through football.
3. RESPONSIBILITIES-Hook areas.
4. TECHNIQUES-Zone coverage.
5. REACTIONS-Cover hooks

These defensive adjustments against the pro-sets also handles play action passes from the basic veer backfield patterns.

12

ADJUSTING THE COMBO DEFENSE TO THE DOUBLE WINGED T

APPLYING THE COMBO SYSTEM
VS. DOUBLE WINGED T OFFENSES

Variations of Double Winged offenses have been around for a long time. They originally were used as supplementary formations with both the old singlewing and "T" formations. It is common today to find them as the basic formation used for a balanced running and passing offensive system. Emphasis is usually placed on passing along with a simplified running attack. The advantages are four potential pass receivers are set in positions to quickly get out on their pass patterns along with related running series. The disadvantages are the running sequences usually required the flankers or slots to be in motion before the snap of the ball, and the elimination of the quick dive plays reduces the pressure on the defensive interior fronts. The formation causes the defense to think pass first, and motion can change the defensive thinking to run before the snap. The motion is usually from the backside to the frontside of the backfield patterns.

CHARACTERISTICS OF THE DOUBLE WINGED T OFFENSES

The double winged T offensive systems can either be called in series or number their backs. They combine fullback belly and cross buck series along with four-man pass patterns. They combine straight-on and "X" blocking schemes, with the offensive tackle very often making the calls. Double slot formations force the defensive alignments to adjust to two split sides. The defensive adjustments to a single split side slot was covered in Chapter 9, and adjustments to a single tight side flanker was covered in Chapter 11. A double slot presents two split sides which results in a variation of defensive adjustments and alignments.

FIGURE 12-1 Shows the four basic formations that are commonly used in double winged offensive attacks. Not shown, is a double winged flanker with two tight sides, because it is rarely seen.

The top two diagrams show a slot to one side, and a flanker to the other. The top left panel shows the slot to the right split side, and the flanker to the left tight side. The top right panel shows the slot to the left split side, and the flanker to the right tight side. The adjustments for defensive alignments

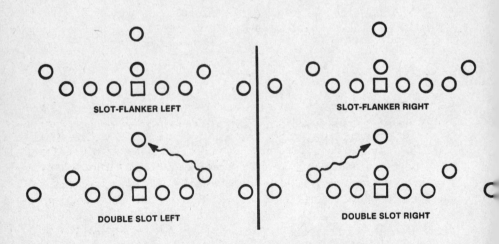

Figure 12-1
Basic Double Winged T Formations

against these offensive lines have already been covered in Chapters 9 and 11.

The bottom two diagrams show double slots with motion. The defense can use the motion to determine the backsides and frontsides of the formations before the snap. The bottom left panel shows the offensive frontside to the defense's left, and the bottom right panel shows the offense's frontside to the right. These are the two more popular formations, and what we will adjust our defenses against, since they will cause a variation in our defensive alignments. If there is no motion then our defense will not need to make pre-snap set adjustments, they will react from their basic sets.

FIGURE 12-2 Shows the basic running sequences from the double slot formations to both the left and the right. There are variations of sweeps, slants, fullback traps up the middle, and inside slot back reverses used for running plays. They feature playaction passes with motion, and drop back passes with four receivers out on patterns. The following descriptions are the plays and their variations in sequence.

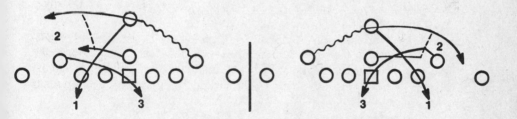

Figure 12-2
Basic Double Winged T Series

1. The first plays in series are hand-offs to the fullback off tackle behind crossblocking. After the quarterback completes his hand-offs, he fakes on the pitch out option to the slot in motion. The second variations in sequence are to hand-off to the fullback up the middle behind short traps, before faking a slant to the slot in motion.

2. The second plays in series are the pitchout options to the slot in motion after faking the fullback handoffs. The second variations in sequence are outside hand offs to the slot in motion on slants after faking the fullback short traps. The third variation are pitchouts to the slot in motion behind sweep blocking.

3. The third plays in series are the inside reverses through center behind the traps of the frontside pulling tackles.

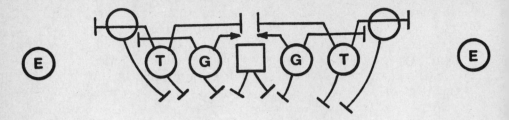

Figure 12-3
Basic X Blocking System

FIGURE 12-3 Shows the basic X (cross) blocking system used with double slots. The numbers for the point of attack are usually used on the defensive linemen instead of the offensive linemen, with the offensive tackles very often making the calls for either straight on or cross blocking. The offensive call men block down, with their inside adjacent linemen blocking out at the point of attacks. The frontside offensive tackles usually pull toward the backside to trap over center. Regardless of the numbering system or blocking rules that are applied to X (cross) blocking, the principles are still basically the same.

ADJUSTING THE COMBO SYSTEM
TO DOUBLE SLOT TACTICAL TENDENCIES

In order to adjust our defense for sets, keys, and responsibilities we must take into consideration that two split sides leave one less hole through which to run, and we must balance our alignments to their balanced sets to quickly pick-up all four pass receivers. Only their motion will eliminate the threat of one of those receivers, and we can make our set adjustments with pre-snap invert rotation to their motion. Since there is no tight end our tight cornerback will share the same duties as the split cornerback on the other side. Our defensive alignments will be balanced with a tight Eagle set on 53 calls, and a double stack on 44 calls. The safety and backside cornerback will pre rotate with motion. Basic techniques and reactions will be applied, and this will be our basic approach for both 53 and 44 defensive call.

FIGURES 12-4 and 12-5 show our set adjustments, keys, and responsibilities against the double slot with both 53 and 44 calls. The split corner-back will set to the left outside heel of his left defensive end, and the tight cornerback will set to the right outside heel of his right defensive end. They will both key their respective offensive slot backs.

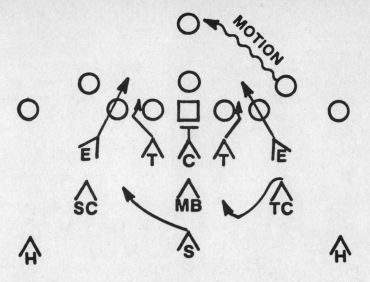

Figure 12-4
53 Call

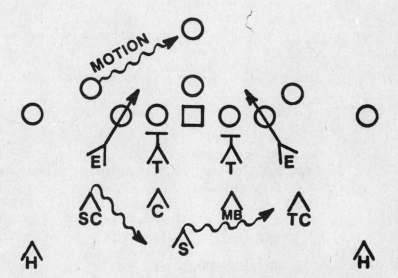

Figure 12-5
44 Call

53 CALL (Figure 12-4) shows the right slot in motion to our left. The safety begins his pre snap rotation towards Dog, and the tight cornerback begins his pre snap rotation towards Baker. Both ends crash through the sets of the offensive tackles with inside shoulder contact on the quarterback. Both tackles set shading the outside shoulders of the offensive guards, and apply forearm shiver reach techniques on the offensive tackles before getting control of the guard tackle gaps. The combo is the nose man on center getting forearm shiver control handling both inside guard gaps. The middle linebacker plays football, and our two halfbacks use zone coverage.

44 CALL (Figure 12-5) shows the left slot in motion to our right. The safety begins his pre snap rotation to Easy, and the split cornerback begins his pre snap rotation towards Baker. Both tackles set head on their offensive guard, with forearm shiver control against pressure. Both inside linebackers stack their defensive tackles and play football. Our two halfbacks use zone coverage.

INDIVIDUAL ADJUSTMENTS AGAINST
THE DOUBLE SLOT "T" RUNNING SERIES

The individual sets, keys, responsibilities, techniques, and reactions are shown and explained for each position against each double slot T play. The 53 calls willl be applied in the left panels, and the 44 calls will be applied in the right panels as follows:

FIGURES 12-6 and 12-7 show the fullback bellies run outside tackle behind cross blocking.

53 Call vs. double slot f. b. belly to our left (Figure 12-6)

ENDS: (BOTH LEFT AND RIGHT)

1. SETS-Outside and facing through their offensive tackles.
2. KEYS-Quarterback.
3. RESPONSIBILITIES-Force the play maintaining inside shoulder pursuit to the quarterback.
4. TECHNIQUES-Charge through tackles' sets beating the slotback blocking angles to positions of contact and control.
5. REACTIONS-Contact guard on pull, and trail motion.

TACKLES: (BOTH LEFT AND RIGHT)

1. SETS-Shade outside shoulders of offensive guards.
2. KEYS-Fullback and ball.
3. RESPONSIBILITIES-Outside guard gaps.

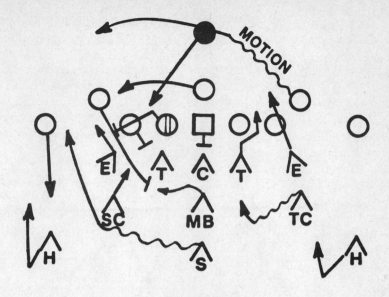

Figure 12-6
53 Call

4. TECHNIQUES-Forearm shiver reach on offensive tackles.
5. REACTIONS-Neutralize and control inside tackle.

COMBO (NOSE GUARD)

1. SET-Head up, on offensive center.
2. KEY-Center's hand and ball.
3. RESPONSIBILITIES-Both center and guard gaps.
4. TECHNIQUE-Forearm shiver control on center reading his head.
5. REACTION-Fight pressure to the left.

MIDDLE LINEBACKER:

1. SET-Stacks behind combo.
2. KEY-Reads fullback and football.
3. RESPONSIBILITIES-Lateral pursuit, frontside hook area.
4. TECHNIQUE-Play the football.
5. REACTION-Left pursuit.

CORNERBACKS (SPLIT LEFT AND TIGHT RIGHT)

1. SETS-Outside heels of their respective defensive ends.
2. KEYS-Read their respective slot backs.
3. RESPONSIBILITIES-If slot back blocks down the fill and if he goes in motion they rotate to Baker.
4. TECHNIQUES-Zone coverage.
5. REACTIONS-Fill left, and rotate to Baker with left motion.

SAFETY:

1. SET-Middle deep Baker.
2. KEY-Both slotbacks.
3. RESPONSIBILITIES-Offensive flow.
4. TECHNIQUE-Play football.
5. REACTION-Rotate left with motion, and back up the split cornerback.

HALFBACKS: (BOTH LEFT AND RIGHT)

Zones: Sets, Keys, responsibilities, techniques, and reactions for Charlie and Able respectively.

44 Call vs. double slot f.b. belly to our right (Figure 12-7)

ENDS: (BOTH LEFT AND RIGHT)

1. SETS-Outside and facing through their offensive tackles.
2. KEYS-Quarterback.
3. RESPONSIBILITIES-Force the play maintaining inside shoulder pursuit to the quarterback.
4. TECHNIQUES-Charge through tackles' sets beating the slot backs' blocking angles to positions of contact and control.
5. REACTIONS-Trail motion, and contract guard on pull.

TACKLES: (BOTH LEFT AND RIGHT)

1. SETS-Shade outside shoulders of offensive guards.
2. KEYS-Fullback and ball.
3. RESPONSIBILITIES-Outside guard gaps.
4. TECHNIQUES-Forearm shiver reach on offensive tackles.
5. REACTIONS-Neutralize and control inside tackles.

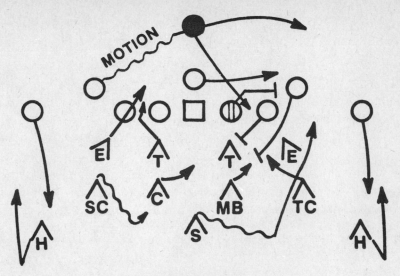

Figure 12-7
44 Call

INTERIOR LINEBACKERS: (COMBO AND MIDDLE LINEBACKER)

1. SETS-Stacks defensive tackles.
2. KEYS-Read fullback and football.
3. RESPONSIBILITIES-Lateral pursuit.
4. TECHNIQUES-Play football.
5. REACTIONS-Combo backup middle linebacker right.

CORNERBACKS (BOTH SPLIT AND TIGHT)

1. SETS-Outside heels of respective defensive ends.
2. KEYS-Read their respective slotbacks.
3. RESPONSIBILITIES-If slotback blocks down they fill, and if he goes in motion they rotate to Baker.
4. TECHNIQUES-Zone coverage.
5. REACTIONS-Rotate to Baker with right motion, fill right.

SAFETY:

1. SET-Middle deep Baker.

2. KEY-Both slotbacks.
3. RESPONSIBILITIES-Offensive flow.
4. TECHNIQUE-Play football.
5. REACTION-Rotate right with motion, and back up tight corner-back.

HALFBACKS: (BOTH LEFT AND RIGHT)

Zones: Sets, keys, responsibilities, techniques and reactions for Charlie and Able respectively.

FIGURES 12-8 and 12-9 show the option being run from the double slot with motion after a fake to the fullback. The sets, keys, responsibilities, and techniques, for all positions remain basically the same as in Figures 12-6 and 12-7. The only variations are the final reactions to the differences in the plays. We will only cover the reactions of each position to the plays to prevent repetition.

53 Call vs. double slot option to our left (Figure 12-8)

LEFT END: Close down on quarterback and pulling guard forcing a quick pitchout.

RIGHT END: Crash through the defensive tackle with a cut-off angle on

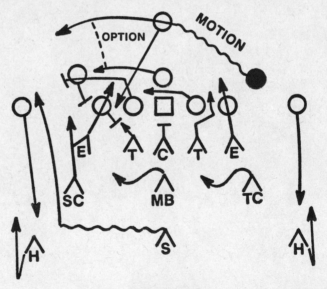

Figure 12-8
53 Call

the slot in motion trying to get him from behind if he receives the pitchout.

LEFT TACKLE: Meet the tackle's lead block to neutralize the outside position of the hole.

RIGHT TACKLE: Inside tackle control, left pursuit.

COMBO: Neutralize and control center, fight pressure to our left.

SPLIT CORNERBACK: Fill left behind their slotback blocking down.

MIDDLE LINEBACKER: Play football and flow to our left.

TIGHT CORNERBACK: Pre rotate with motion to our left, and Baker zone coverage.

SAFETY: Pre rotate with motion to our left, and then come up to fill with outside containment.

LEFT HALFBACK: Charlie zone coverage.

RIGHT HALFBACK: Able zone coverage.

44 Call vs. double slot option to our right (Figure 12-9)

LEFT END: Crash through the defensive tackle with a cut-off angle on the slot in motion trying to get him from behind if he receives the pitchout.

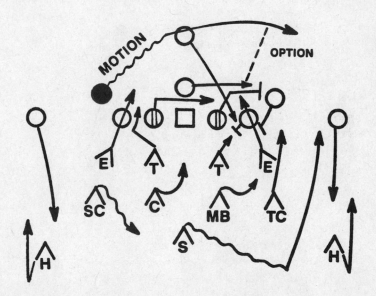

Figure 12-9

RIGHT END: Close down on quarterback and pulling guard forcing a quick pitchout.

LEFT TACKLE: Inside tackle control, right pursuit.

RIGHT TACKLE: Meet the tackles lead block to neutralize the outside postition of the hole.

COMBO: Back up the middle linebacker to the right preventing a cut back.

MIDDLE LINEBACKER: Play football and flow to the right.

SPLIT CORNERBACK: Pre rotate with motion to our right, and Baker zone coverage.

TIGHT CORNERBACK: Fill right behind their slotback blocking down.

SAFETY: Pre rotate with motion to our right, and then come up to fill with outside containment.

LEFT HALFBACK: Charlie zone coverage.

RIGHT HALFBACK: Able zone coverage.

FIGURES 12-10 and 12-11 show the inside slot back reverses being run behind the tackles' traps. Again the sets, keys, responsibilities, and techniques for all positions are basically the same. Their following reactions to reverses should and will vary based on their keys.

53 Calls vs. inside slotback reverse to our right (Figure 12-10)

LEFT END: Crash through with the pulling offensive tackle hitting the quarterback before the fullback can fake and block him.

RIGHT END: Charge with motion preventing wide path on reverse.

LEFT TACKLE: Reach on offensive tackle, and follow through.

RIGHT TACKLE: Reach and close down.

COMBO: FIGHT DOUBLE TEAM pressure to right.

SPLIT CORNERBACK: Go with slotback, and prevent his cutback on reverse. Yell "reverse!"

MIDDLE LINEBACKER: Must cover backfield pattern to left.

TIGHT CORNERBACK: Pre rotation with motion to our left, fill reverse hole.

SAFETY: Pre rotation with motion to our left, Baker zone coverage.

LEFT HALFBACK: Charlie zone coverage.

RIGHT HALFBACK: Able zone coverage.

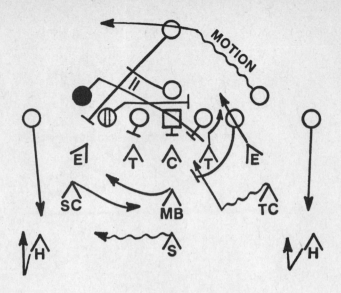

Figure 12-10
53 Call

44 Call vs. inside slotback reverse to our left (Figure 12-11)

LEFT END: Charge with motion preventing wide path on reverse.

RIGHT END: Crash through with the pulling offensive tackle hitting the quarterback before the fullback can fake and block him.

LEFT TACKLE: Close down on trap.

RIGHT TACKLE: Fight pressure to left.

COMBO: Fill reverse hole.

MIDDLE LINEBACKER: Cover backfield pattern to right.

SPLIT CORNERBACK: Pre rotate with motion to our right, fill reverse hole.

TIGHT CORNERBACK: Go with slotback and prevent his cutback on reverse. Yell "Reverse."

SAFETY: Pre rotation with motion to our right, Baker zone coverage.

LEFT HALFBACK: Charlie zone coverage.

RIGHT HALFBACK: Able zone coverage.

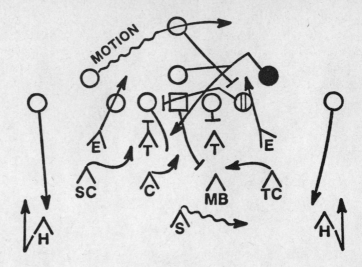

Figure 12-11
44 Call

We have shown both 53 and 44 Defenses against the double slot T offenses. Because our defense needs to be in position to cover four receivers before any offensive pre-snap motion, the 44 calls will be our primary alignments, and the 53 calls will be our secondary alignments.

SECONDARY ADJUSTMENTS AGAINST
THE DOUBLE SLOT PASSING GAME

With motion our defense is no different against the Double Slot T than any other winged T with play action or bootleg passes. With the Double Slot T, before motion, we must worry about the fourth receiver without a playaction fake. This is why we must be set in a defensive alignment ready for four receivers before the motion. After the motion we can make our pre snap adjustments, and be in a position to react to their backfield patterns with only three receivers out. This includes their swing man, or the fourth man out of the backfield. We want to be in a position both before the snap and after the snap to react to our responsibilities. Those responsibilities are naturally based on keys.

Our ends and tackles apply their basic containment and pass rush. The set, keys, responsibilities, techniques, and reactions of each position of our pass defenders will be covered. These positions are: the two halfbacks, safety, split cornerback, tight cornerback, combo, and middle linebacker.

FIGURES 12-12 and 12-13 show the Double slot T passes run without a fake, and four receivers out on a pattern. They are being run against our 53 defense to the left, and our 44 defense to the right.

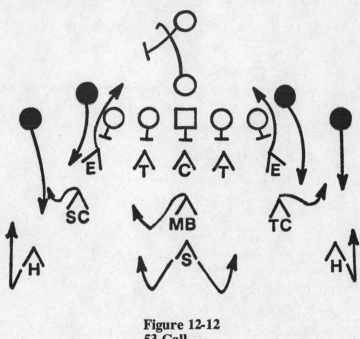

Figure 12-12
53 Call

53 Call vs. double slot T dropback passes (Figure 12-12)

HALFBACKS: (BOTH LEFT AND RIGHT)

1. SETS-10 to 12 yards, outside deep zones.
2. KEYS-Outside receivers, split ends.
3. RESPONSIBILITIES-Charlie and Able zones respectively.
4. TECHNIQUES-Zone coverage.
5. REACTIONS-Cover split ends deep.

SAFETY:

1. SET-Middle deep Baker.
2. KEY-Both slotbacks.
3. RESPONSIBILITIES-Baker zone.
4. TECHNIQUE-Zone coverage.
5. REACTION-Protect zone.

CORNERBACKS: (SPLIT LEFT AND TIGHT RIGHT)

1. SETS-Outside heels of their respective defensive ends.
2. KEYS-Read their respective slotbacks.
3. RESPONSIBILITIES-Dog and Easy flats respectively.
4. TECHNIQUES-Zone coverage.
5. REACTIONS-Protect zones.

MIDDLE LINEBACKER

1. SET-Stacked behind combo (nose guard).
2. KEY-Reads fullback and football.
3. RESPONSIBILITIES-Hook areas.
4. TECHNIQUE-Zone coverage.
5. REACTION-Left hook area with fullback.

44 Call vs. double slot T dropback passes (Figure 12-13)

HALFBACKS: (BOTH LEFT AND RIGHT)

1. SETS-10 to 12 yard outside deep zones.
2. KEYS-Outside receivers, split ends.
3. RESPONSIBILITIES-Charlie and Able zones respectively.
4. TECHNIQUES-Zone coverage.
5. REACTIONS-Cover split ends deep.

SAFETY:

1. SET-Middle deep Baker.
2. KEY-Both slotbacks.
3. RESPONSIBILITIES-Baker zone.
4. TECHNIQUE-Zone coverage.
5. REACTION-Protect zone.

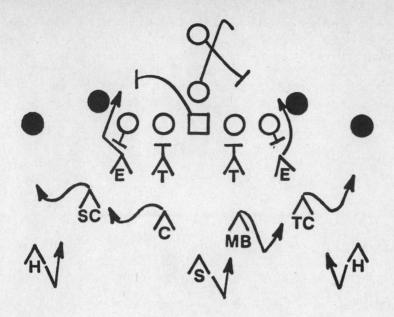

Figure 12-13

CORNERBACKS: (SPLIT LEFT AND TIGHT RIGHT)

1. SETS-Outside heels of respective defensive ends.
2. KEYS-Read their respective slotbacks.
3. RESPONSIBILITIES-Dog and Easy flats respectively.
4. TECHNIQUES-Zone coverage.
5. REACTIONS-Protect zones.

INTERIOR LINEBACKERS (COMBO LEFT AND MIDDLE RIGHT)

1. SETS-Stacked behind their respective defensive tackles.
2. KEYS-Reads fullback and football.
3. RESPONSIBILITIES-Dog and Easy hook areas.
4. TECHNIQUES-Zone coverage.
5. REACTIONS-Respective hook areas.

This completes our defensive adjustments against the Double Slot T formation. It has been our experience that when we defense Double Winged formations with a slot to one side, and a flanker to the other, they usually have definite tactical tendencies. The motion and passing usually comes from the slot side, and they usually favor to run toward the flanker side. The flanker is used on reverses so they will have a tight end for a cut off block where offensive tackle pulls on his trap.

13

ATTACKING THE UNBALANCED SINGLE WING WITH THE COMBO

APPLYING THE COMBO SYSTEM VS. THE UNBALANCED SINGLE WING

The Single Wing was a popular offense during the late 20's, 30's and early 40's before it gave away to the "T" formations. Today, it is almost totally extinct at the pro or college levels. High school coaches will occasionally meet an opponent who uses it. Because it is so unfamiliar and different from their usual week-to-week defensive preparation, coaches will have the nightmare of spending much extra time getting ready for it. It is sometimes run behind a balanced line; but it is the unbalanced lines that increase the defensive problems. There are a few Winged "T" systems (Chapter 8) that run behind those unbalanced lines. Its advantages are an alignment for

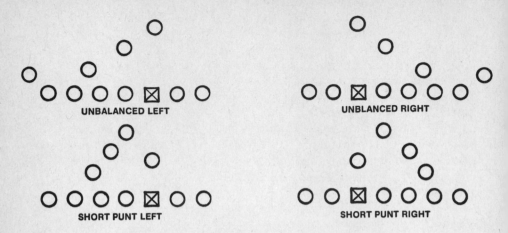

Figure 13-1
Basic Unbalanced Single Wing Formations

punishing double team blocks on the defensive players at all points of attack, the defenses are usually not familiar with it, and it presents a triple threat with the addition of the quick kick. Its disadvantages are: the center has to look between his legs to snap the ball, the plays are slow developing with emphasis on power, and it is stereo-typed as being old fashioned by fans. They like the direct exchange between a quarterback under center as a starting point to follow the ball throughout the play. The public very often feels the singlewing is tactically unsound in modern football. Any defensive coach who might feel this way will set himself up for the shock of his professional life.

CHARACTERISTICS OF THE UNBALANCED SINGLEWING

Most all singlewing systems call their plays in series without numbering their backs. They run power tandems, spinner, and bucklateral plays behind post and lead blocking. This blocking results in double team and seal blocks to the inside of the point of attack, with tandem traps to the outside of the holes. Singlewing emphasizes power without tactical speed, which physically punishes the defense. The most outstanding characteristic is that the center snaps the ball between his legs to a back set from three and a half yards to five yards deep. This technique is not as difficult as it may seem as long as the snap is soft, and knee level or below. A high snap will raise the back up from a low two point stance, destroying their timing. A well schooled singlewing team will be as consistent with their snap as a T formation exchange, even though the center has to look between his legs, and usually has a defensive nose man on him. Actually, the singlewing tailback has much more time to recover and follow through with a bad exchange.

FIGURE 13-1 Shows the basic singlewing formations behind unbalanced lines. The two top diagrams behind unbalanced lines to our left (panel), and our right (panel). The singlewing feature a tailback set five yards behind center and a fullback set four and a half yards behind the strongside guard. The center can make a direct snap to either the tailback or fullback. A blocking back is set behind the strongside tackle, and the wingback flanks the strongside end.

The two bottom diagrams show the short punt formations set behind unbalanced lines. They were supplementary formations used with the singlewing, and were more commonly used with balance singlewing.

FIGURE 13-2 Shows the three basic singlewing sequences run to both the left and right. These are plays that feature the tandem power, spinner, and. bucklateral series.

1. The top two diagrams show the basic power tamdem series run unbalanced to our left in the left panel, and unbalanced to our right in the right panel. The tailback takes the direct snap and carries behind the tandem-traps and seals of the blocking back and pulling guards to the strongside. The fullback takes the snap and makes an inside hand-off to the wingback behind the tandem trap and seals of the blocking back and pulling guards to the shortside.

2. The middle two diagrams show the four play sequence of the buck lateral series run unbalanced to our left (panel) and right (panel). The first play the fullback takes a direct snap and fakes to the spinning blocking back on an inside trap up the middle. The second play the fullback hands off to the spinning blocking back who pitches out behind sweep blocking. The third play the blocking back fakes the pitchout before spinning back behind trap blocking over his tackle hole. The fourth play the blocking back makes an outside hand-off to the wingback behind trap blocking to the shortside.

3. The bottom two diagrams show the three play spinner series from the short punt being run to the shortside of unbalanced lines to both the left and right. The first play is the hand-off to the tailback on a trap up the middle after faking a slant. The second play is to hand-off on the slant to the short side behind sweep trap blocking before faking to the tailback up the middle. The third play is to spin and keep the strongside behind trap blocking.

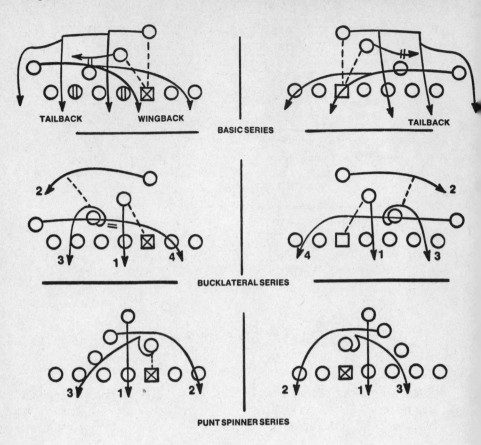

Figure 13-2
Basic Single Wing Series

FIGURE 13-3 Shows the basic post and lead blocking system used with the unbalanced singlewing. The center of the line is set on the strong side guard to fix the positions in the line so they can have one set of balanced blocking rules of the strongside guard to middle guard with their odd holes to the left, and even holes to the right. The tackle and center are set to either side of the middle guard. These are the only two positions that are flip-flopped, and this determines which side is unbalanced left or right. If it is unbalanced left the center is to the right and the tackle is to the left of the middle guard. This fixes the sets of all their pulling linemen. The middle guard can pull

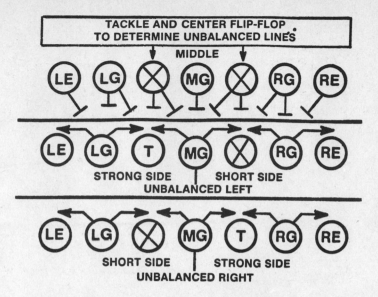

Figure 13-3
Post and Lead Blocking System for Unbalanced Lines

either way and trap or lead on wide holes. The left or right guards can pull and trap on inside holes, and seal on wide holes. There is always a double team block and seal to the inside of the points-of-attacked called.

ADJUSTING THE COMBO SYSTEM
TO SINGLEWING TACTICAL TENDENCIES

In order to adjust our defense for sets, keys, and responsibilities we will consider their strongside guard in the same way as we would a center, the strongside as the tight side, and the short side as the split side. This will basically shift our 53 defense down one and a half man, and the 44 defense down one full man. It will always assure us that we will have a down defensive lineman on their center who is looking between his legs before the snap. Trying to control the line-of-scrimmage with our basic techniques for position alone could give their offensive plays the time they need to develop. We must penetrate the line-of-scrimmage with more stunts than usual to prevent them from gaining momentum. This can be backed up with man-to-man pass coverage. Our halfback to their strongside can play their wingback, and our

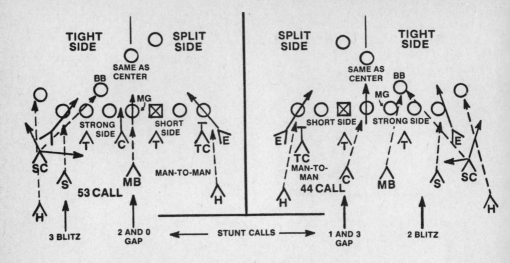

Figure 13-4
Set Adjustments and Keys vs. Unbalanced Lines

halfback to their shortside can play their backside end. Our split cornerback sets to the wingback's side and keys their wingback through to their blocking back. Our tight cornerback applys his bump and recovery techniques on their shortside end. Our interior linebackers key and play their middle offensive guard and blocking back.

FIGURE 13-4 shows our set adjustments, keys, and responsibilities against the single wing with a 53 call in the left panel, and a 44 call in the right panel:

53 CALL against a singlewing unbalanced to our left shows our split cornerback set to our left reading and reacting through their wingback to the blocking back. Our safety keys and reacts to their left strongside end man-to-man. Our tight cornerback applies his basic bump and recovery technique on their shortside end to the right. The middle linebacker keys and plays their middle guard. Our left halfback plays their wingback, and our right halfback plays their shortside end. Our right tackle plays noseman on their center. We apply 2 and 0 gap calls on stunts, and a 3 gap call on a safety blitz.

44 CALL against a single wing unbalanced to our right shows our split cornerback set to our right reading and reacting through their wingback to the blocking back. Our safety keys and reacts to their right strongside end man-to-man. Our tight cornerback applies his basic bump and recovery technique on their shortside end to the left. The combo plays the offensive middle, and the middle linebacker plays the blocking back. Our left halfback plays their shortside end, and our right halfback plays their wingback. Our left tackle plays noseman on their center. We apply 1 and 3 gap calls on stunts, and a 2 gap call on a safety blitz.

INDIVIDUAL ADJUSTMENTS AGAINST THE SINGLEWING RUNNING ATTACK

The individual sets, keys, responsibilities, techniques, and reactions are shown and explained for each position against the single wing plays. The 53 calls will be applied to our left, and the 44 calls will be covered to the right as follows.

FIGURES 13-5 and 13-6 show the basic tandem-trap plays being run to both the strongside and shortside.

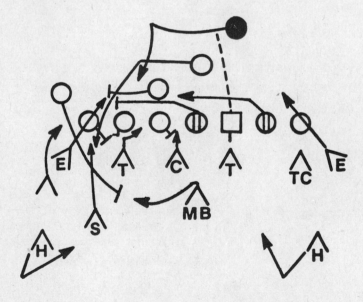

Figure 13-5
53 Call

53 Call vs. tailback tandem trap to our left (Figure 13-5)

LEFT END:

1. SET-Outside and facing through their strongside end.
2. KEY-Blocking back.
3. RESPONSIBILITIES-Close down outside tackle holes.
4. TECHNIQUE-Charge through strongside end's set, using both forearms to split tandem.
5. REACTION-Split tandem trap up on contact.

RIGHT END:

1. SET-Outside facing through their shortside end.
2. KEY-Blocking back.
3. RESPONSIBILITIES-Close down outside tackle holes.
4. TECHNIQUE-Charge through shortside end's set.
5. REACTION-Trail, trying to catch the tailback from behind.

LEFT TACKLE:

1. SET-On strongside left guard.
2. KEY-Read his head.
3. RESPONSIBILITIES-Neutralize double teams
4. TECHNIQUE-Forearm shiver control.
5. REACTION-Fight pressure to left.

RIGHT TACKLE:

1. SET-Head on center who is looking between his legs.
2. KEY-Movement of ball.
3. RESPONSIBILITIES-Gaps to both sides of center.
4. TECHNIQUE-Forearm shiver control.
5. REACTION-Fight pressure to left

COMBO:

1. SET-Gap between their strongside tackle and guard.
2. KEY-Movement.
3. RESPONSIBILITIES-Penetration.
4. TECHNIQUE-Shoot the gap.
5. REACTION-Grab legs.

MIDDLE LINEBACKER:

1. SET-Over offensive middle guard, off the L.O.S.
2. KEY-Middle guard through to blocking back.
3. RESPONSIBILITIES-Pursuit, strongside hook area.
4. TECHNIQUE-Play football.
5. REACTION-Left.

SPLIT CORNERBACK:

1. SET-Strongside left, outside heel of defensive end.
2. KEY-Read wingback through to the blocking back.
3. RESPONSIBILITES-Outside containment, Dog zone.
4. TECHNIQUE-Come up with controlled hitting position.
5. REACTION-Fill with wingback blocking down.

TIGHT CORNERBACK:

1. SET-On shortside end to our right.
2. KEY-End's movement.
3. RESPONSIBILITIES-Outside containment, Easy zone.
4. TECHNIQUE-Bump and recovery.
5. REACTION-Easy zone coverage.

SAFETY:

1. SET-6 to 8 yard off their strongside end to our left.
2. KEY-End's movement.
3. RESPONSIBILITIES-Play end, Baker.
4. TECHNIQUE-Man-to-man.
5. REACTION-Come up and fill behind the blocking down of the strongside end.

LEFT HALFBACK:

1. SET-10 to 12 yards off their wingback to our left.
2. KEY-Wingback.
3. RESPONSIBILITIES-Charlie zone.
4. TECHNIQUE-Man-to-man coverage.
5. REACTION-When wingback blocks down back up safety with outside containment.

RIGHT HALFBACK:

1. SET-10 to 12 yards off their shortside end to our right.
2. KEY-Blocking back.
3. RESPONSIBILITIES-Able zone.
4. TECHNIQUE-Man-to-man.
5. REACTION-Left back up.

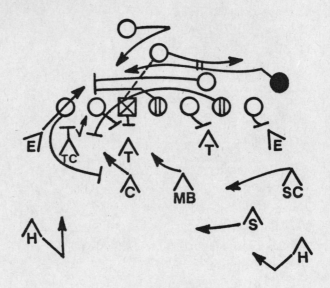

Figure 13-6
44 Call

44 Call vs. wingback tandem trap to our left (Figure 13-6)

LEFT END:

1. SET-Outside facing through their shortside end.
2. KEY-Blocking back.
3. RESPONSIBILITIES-Close down outside tackle holes.
4. TECHNIQUE-Charge through shortside ends' set.
5. REACTION-Split tandem trap upon contact.

RIGHT END:

1. SET-Outside facing through their strongside end.

2. KEY-Blocking back.
3. RESPONSIBILITIES-Close down outside tackle holes.
4. TECHNIQUE-Charge through strongside ends set.
5. REACTION-Trail trying to get the wingback from behind.

LEFT TACKLE:

1. SET-Head on center who is looking between his legs.
2. KEY-Movement of ball.
3. RESPONSIBILITIES-Gap to both sides of center.
4. TECHNIQUE-Forearm shiver control.
5. REACTION-Neutralize double team to his left.

RIGHT TACKLE:

1. SET-Shade inside shoulder of strongside guard to our right.
2. KEY-Read his head.
3. RESPONSIBILITIES-Tackle guard gap control.
4. TECHNIQUE-Force arm shiver control.
5. REACTION-Left with pulling guard.

COMBO:

1. SET-Stack his defensive left tackle (nose man).
2. KEY-Middle guard.
3. RESPONSIBILITIES-Pursuit, left hook area.
4. TECHNIQUE-Play football.
5. REACTION-Left with pulling middle guard.

MIDDLE LINEBACKER:

1. SET-Over offensive tackle off the L.O.S.
2. KEY-Blocking back.
3. RESPONSIBILITIES-Pursuit, right hook area.
4. TECHNIQUE-Play football.
5. REACTION-Left with blocking back.

SPLIT CORNERBACK:

1. SET-Strongside right, outside heel of defensive end.
2. KEY-Read wingback through to the blocking back.
3. RESPONSIBILITIES-Outside containment, Easy zone.

4. TECHNIQUE-Pursuit.

5. REACTION- Left.

TIGHT CORNERBACK:

1. SET-On shortside end to our left.

2. KEY-End's movement.

3. RESPONSIBILITIES-Neutralize end forcing him to the outside with inside control.

4. TECHNIQUE-Bump and recovery.

5. REACTION-Inside control and fill.

SAFETY:

1. SET-6 to 8 yards off the shortside end to our right.

2. KEY-End's movement.

3. RESPONSIBILITIES-Play end, Baker.

4. TECHNIQUE-Man-to-man.

5. REACTION-Cover Baker.

HALFBACKS: (BOTH LEFT AND RIGHT)

The same as it was with the 53 defense.

FIGURES 13-7 and *13-8* show the bucklateral series being run from the unbalanced singlewing set to both our left and right. The sets, keys, responsibilities, and techniques for all positions remain basically the same as in Figured 13-5 and 13-6. The only variations are the final reactions of each position to the differences in the plays. We will only cover the reactions of each position to the play to prevent repetition.

53 CALL VS. BUCKLATERAL SERIES
UNBALANCED TO OUR LEFT (FIGURE 13-7)

The fullback takes a direct snap from center and hands off to the spinning blocking back before continuing his fake up the middle. The blocking back either pitches out, or keeps the ball spinning back over his tackle. He can lateral the ball to the trailing tailback after they have cleared the line-of-scrimmage. The following defensive reactions are for each position.

LEFT END Charge through the set of their strongside end making contact with the pulling middle guard, and closing down on the blocking back.

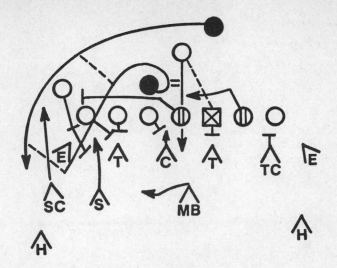

Figure 13-7
53 Call

RIGHT END Charge through the set of their short side end trailing the pulling right guard to try and make the play from behind.

LEFT TACKLE Neutralize and fight through their double team block to our left.

RIGHT TACKLE Hit the center and fill the gap to the left.

COMBO Shoot the gap and mess up the exchange between their fullback and blocking back.

SPLIT CORNERBACK When the wingback blocks down, go up to meet the tailback on outside containment.

MIDDLE LINEBACK Pursue left.

TIGHT CORNERBACK Hit end easy coverage.

SAFETY When their strongside end blocks down fill behind him.

LEFT HALFBACK Backs up split cornerback.

RIGHT HALFBACK Able zone coverage.

44 CALL VS. BUCKLATERAL SERIES
UNBALANCED TO OUR RIGHT (FIGURE 13-8)

The fullback takes a direct snap from center and either hands-off to the

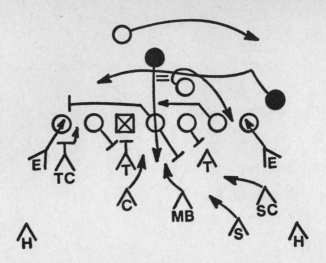

Figure 13-8
44 Call

spinning blocking back or keeps it up the middle. If the blocking back gets the ball he makes an outside hand off to his wingback, before carrying out his fake with the tailback to our right.

> *LEFT END* Charge through the set of their shortside end making contact with the pulling guard, and closing down on the wingback.
>
> *RIGHT END* Charge through the set of their strongside end trailing the wingback and try to tackle him from behind.
>
> *LEFT TACKLE* Hit the center, and neutralize the double team block to the left.
>
> *RIGHT TACKLE* React left with the pulling guard fighting through the block.
>
> *COMBO* If middle guard pulls react left, and if he blocks down, fill and hit the fullback.
>
> *MIDDLE LINEBACKER* Fill the center, and hit the fullback.
>
> *SPLIT CORNERBACK* Left pursuit with wingback.
>
> *TIGHT CORNERBACK* Fill the hole after inside recovery.
>
> *SAFETY* Short Baker.

LEFT HALFBACK Backs up tight cornerback.

RIGHT HALFBACK Able zone coverage.

FIGURES 13-9 and *13-10* show the spinner series being run from shortpunt to the shortside of unbalanced lines to both our left and right. Again the sets, keys, responsibilities, and techniques are still the same, and we will only cover the variations in the final reactions for each position. The basic Winged T series (Chapter 8) was an outgrowth of this spinner series. The bootleg replaces the spinner. This is an excellent shortside attack to complement the singlewing. The basic sequence goes to the shortside with a spinner back to the strongside of the unbalanced lines.

53 CALL VS. SPINNER SERIES TO OUR RIGHT (FIGURE 13-9)

The spinning back takes a direct snap and either hands off on a slant, or fakes the hand-off and gives it to the tailback up the middle on a short trap. Their offensive line is unbalanced to our left, and the sequence is run to our right. The following defensive reactions are for each position.

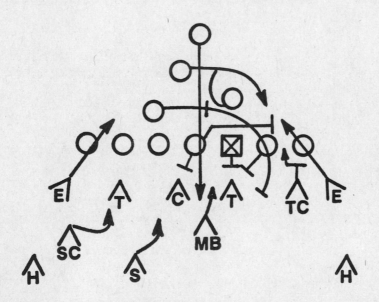

Figure 13-9
53 Call

LEFT END Charge through the set of their strongside end closing down with and inside shoulder relationship to the spinning back.

RIGHT END Charge through the set of their shortside end making contact with the pulling middle guard and closing down the hole with an inside shoulder relationship.

LEFT TACKLE Neutralize their left guard fighting through the reading of his head.

RIGHT TACKLE Hit the center, and fight through their double team block to our right.

COMBO Shoot the gap trying to mess up the timing.

MIDDLE LINEBACKER React right with middle guard if he pulls, or fill the hole behind him if he blocks down.

SPLIT CORNERBACK Dog coverage.

TIGHT CORNERBACK Fill the hole after inside recovery.

SAFETY Short Baker coverage.

LEFT HALFBACK Charlie coverage.

RIGHT HALFBACK Back up the tight cornerback.

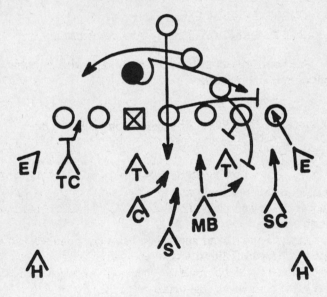

Figure 13-10
44 Call

44 CALL VS. SPINNER SERIES TO OUR LEFT (FIGURE 13-10)

After faking the sequence to our left the spinning back keeps the ball to the right strongside behind trap blocking.

LEFT END Charge through the set of their shortside end closing down the sequence.

RIGHT END Charge through the set of their strongside end making contact with their pulling guard, and closing down the hole with an inside shoulder relationship.

LEFT TACKLE Hit the center, and fight pressure to his right.

RIGHT TACKLE Neutralize the double team block from his right.

COMBO If middle guard pulls react right, and if he blocks down he fills and hits the fullback.

MIDDLE LINEBACKER React with the blocking back and fill behind him to the right.

TIGHT CORNERBACK Dog coverage after recovery.

SPLIT CORNERBACK Fill the hole.

SAFETY Back up the middle linebacker.

LEFT HALFBACK Charlie zone coverage.

RIGHT HALFBACK Back up split cornerback.

This completes both our 53 and 44 defensive adjustments against the singlewing running attack.

SECONDARY ADJUSTMENTS AGAINST THE SINGLEWING PASSING GAME

The singlewing already has their passer set five yards deep with four receivers in pre snap positions to get out on their patterns in a hurry. Our secondary keys and picks them up man-to-man while maintaining zone responsibilities.

Our ends and tackles apply their basic containments and pass rush. The sets, keys, responsibilities, technique, and reactions of each position of our pass defenders will be covered. These positions are: The two halfbacks, safety, split cornerback, tight cornerback, combo, and middle linebacker.

FIGURES 13-11 and *13-12* show singlewing passes being run against a 53 defense to our left, and a 44 defense to our right.

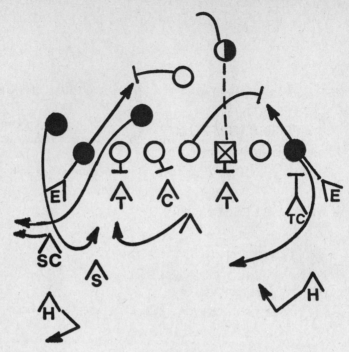

Figure 13-11
53 Call

53 Call vs. singlewing pass strong to our left (Figure 13-11)

LEFT HALFBACK:

1. SET-10 to 12 yards off their wingback.
2. KEY-Wingback.
3. RESPONSIBILITIES-Charlie to Baker zone.
4. TECHNIQUE-Man-to-man.
5. REACTION-Check wingback to hook area, and pick-up strongside end to Charlie.

RIGHT HALFBACK:

1. SET-10 to 12 yards off their shortside end.
2. KEY-Shortside end.
3. RESPONSIBILITIES-Able to Baker zone.

4. TECHNIQUE-Man-to-man.
5. REACTION-Cover the shortside end all the way.

SAFETY:

1. SET-6 to 8 yards off their strongside end.
2. KEY-Strongside end.
3. RESPONSIBILITIES-Baker.
4. TECHNIQUE-Man-to-man.
5. REACTION-Check strongside end to Charlie, cover Baker and back up left hook.

SPLIT CORNERBACK:

1. SET-Strongside left, outside heel of defensive end.
2. KEY-Wingback through to blocking back.
3. RESPONSIBILITIES-Dog flat.
4. TECHNIQUE-Man-to-man.
5. REACTION-Check wingback to hook area, and pick-up blocking back coming into flat.

TIGHT CORNERBACK:

1. SET-On shortside end to our right.
2. KEY-End's movement.
3. RESPONSIBILITIES-Force short side end wide, with inside recovery for Easy zone.
4. TECHNIQUE-Bump and recovery.
5. REACTION-Easy coverage.

COMBO:

1. SET-Left tackle guard gap.
2. KEY-Movement.
3. RESPONSIBILITIES-Gap
4. TECHNIQUE-Charge.
5. REACTION-Pass rush.

MIDDLE LINEBACKER:

1. SET-Over offensive middle guard off the L.O.S.
2. KEY-Blocking back.

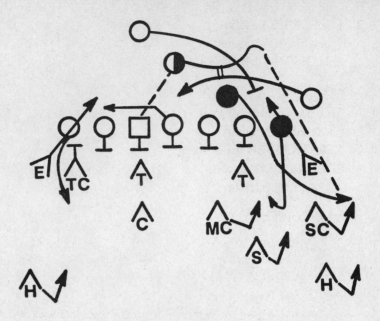

Figure 13-12
44 Call

3. RESPONSIBILITIES-Strongside hook area.
4. TECHNIQUE-Play the football, zone coverage.
5. REACTION-Left hook area.

44 Call vs. fake reverse pass to our right (Figure 13-12)

LEFT HALFBACK:

1. SET-10 to 13 yards off their shortside end.
2. KEY-Shortside end.
3. RESPONSIBILITIES-Charlie to Baker.
4. TECHNIQUE-Man-to-man.
5. REACTION-Cover the shortside end.

RIGHT HALFBACK:

1. SET-10 to 12 yards off their wingback.
2. KEY-Wingback.

3. RESPONSIBILITIES-Able to Baker.

4. TECHNIQUE-Man-to-man.

5. REACTION-Back up split cornerback.

SAFETY:

1. SET-6 to 8 yards off their strongside end.

2. KEY-Shortside end.

3. RESPONSIBILITIES-Baker.

4. TECHNIQUE-Man-to-man.

5. REACTION-Back-up right hook area.

SPLIT CORNERBACK:

1. SET-Strongside right, outside heel of defensive end.

2. KEY-Wingback through to blocking back.

3. RESPONSIBILITIES-Easy flat.

4. TECHNIQUE-Man-to-man.

5. REACTION-Check off from wingback to blocking back, and pick him up in Easy flat.

TIGHT CORNERBACK:

1. SET-On shortside end to our left.

2. KEY-End's movement.

3. RESPONSIBILITIES-Force shortside end wide, with inside recovery for Dog zone.

4. TECHNIQUE-Bump and recovery.

5. REACTION-Dog coverage.

COMBO:

1. SET-Stack his defensive left tackle.

2. KEY-Middle guard through to the blocking back.

3. RESPONSIBILITIES-Running play, left hook area.

4. TECHNIQUE-Play the football zone coverage.

5. REACTION-Play the reverse.

MIDDLE LINEBACKER:

1. SET-Over strongside tackle right off the L.O.S.

2. KEY-Blocking back.

3. RESPONSIBILITIES-Running plays, right hook area.
4. TECHNIQUE-Play the football zone coverage.
5. REACTION-Right hook area.

One of our biggest defensive nightmares was when a smaller school using an unblanced singlewing upset us 19 to 7. The physical beating they gave us was worse than the score. I had come from a singlewing background. As a head coach I failed to convey my respect for their offense to our staff and players. I realized what our attitudes were, and could see it coming: but my efforts to prevent it seemed helpless. When we showed our defensive players their offense, their response was, "Is this all that they do?" We had a defensive coach in making his coaching points say, "It takes a long time for their plays to develop." Though we were tactically prepared, we were not mentally ready. I think that I was the only one in our Camp who was not surprised and shocked. Since the singlewing is different from our normal week-to-week defensive adjustment it is as important to prepare ourselves mentally as it is tactically.

14

HOW TO ADJUST THE COMBO SYSTEM FOR THE SPREADS

APPLYING THE COMBO SYSTEM VS. SPREAD FORMATIONS

A variation of spread formations have always been around, and they all have common tactical approaches based on the same principles. They all put emphasis on the passing game with the passer already set deep, and five receivers in position to get out on their patterns in a hurry. The spread formations very often appear as an element of surprise, and catch defenses unprepared. We spend a few hours in our pre-season practices adjusting our defense against the basic principles of the spread. This is very important if we should get into our season and have an opponent unexpectly use a spread against us. We can immediately call time out, and make our defensive adjustments based on those few hours as a point of reference. The advantages of the spread are: spreading out the defense, passing pressure, and the element of surprise. Its disadvantages are: a limited running attack, inconsistencies for ball control, and clipping penalties from open field play.

CHARACTERISTICS OF THE SPREAD FORMATIONS

There are basically only two types of spread formations: First there are spreads with a combination of double or triple flanker or slot sets to both sides of a balanced line. These were originally known as the "Dutch Meyer," or "Matty Bell" spreads, and are more commonly known today as the "shotgun." It usually has three eligible receivers to one side, and two eligible receivers to the other. The running attack is usually limited to the tailback, along with a possible shovel pass.

The other spreads are variations of an overshift, with the center set to one side of the field on the line-of-scrimmage, and the line set as another unit to the other side. This usually results in four receivers to the one side, with the center being a primary target, and a single receiver or runner behind the line unit to the other side. This was first made popular by George Halas, and became known as the Bear spread. It has since been revised into a system known in some quarters as the "Lonesome Polecat." It is probably more widely known as "The swinging gate spread." This system is much more tactically sound than what might be realized by outside coaches who would regard it as a junk offense. The tailback scrambles are based on priorities and options as a result of defensive reactions. These are definite series of stationary and mobile screens combined with their pass patterns.

These are the only two types of spreads, as long as we take into consideration the variation in the sets of their receivers. We will refer to the balanced spreads as the "Shotgun," and the over shifted spreads as the "Swinging gate."

FIGURE 14-1 shows the "Shotgun" formation. The tailback is set behind his center with both a guard and a tackle set to each of his sides. This gives them a balanced line from which they can apply their basic pass block-

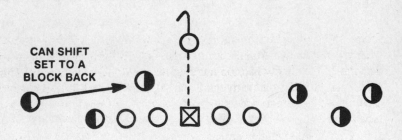

Figure 14-1
The Shotgun Formation

ing. The tailback's set already places him in a position 5 to 7 yards deep from which he can set up very quickly for his pass. They have a split flanker or blocking back, and a tight end set to our left. They have a split slot with a wide flanker set to our right. There could be any number of combinations of double or triple slots and flankers with three receiver to one side and two to the other.

FIGURE 14-2 shows the "Swinging gate" formation. It forces more defensive adjustments than the "Shotgun" does.

Our first experience with the "Swinging gate spread" was in scouting a future opponent playing a much weaker team. With everything to gain and nothing to lose the other team surprised our future opponent with a "Swinging gate spread." As a result, we put our clip boards away, and watched the fireworks. Our future opponent won 41 to 26, and as a result we could not chart their defensive tendencies. A few weeks later we beat them 14 to 13. We had much better offensive personnel than their opponents did; yet we only

Figure 14-2
The Swinging Gate Formation

scored 14 points against them. I would never have courage enough to find out what we could have done, if we had used that offense against them with our personnel. We simply had too much to lose, with nothing to gain. This is the difference in being innovative and stereotyped. Though I have never considered myself as stereotyped as most, I could never have the courage to be that innovative. The lesson I learned was to always be prepared.

The "Swinging gate spread" presents a tailback set 7 to 9 yards behind his center with no pass blockers. The defensive pass rush determines the tailback's options. They have a flanker alignment with two receivers set with their behind the line unit, and they have three eligible receivers (including the

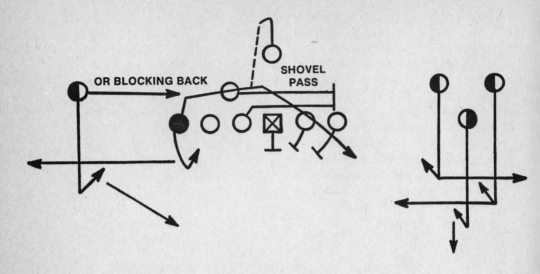

Figure 14-3
The Shotgun Offensive Attack

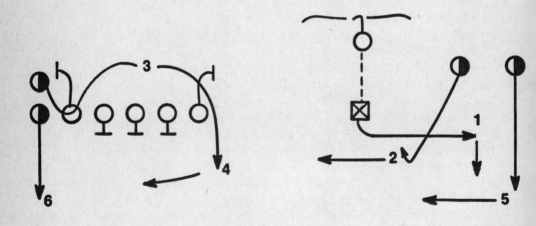

Figure 14-4
The Swinging Gate Offensive Attack

center) to our right. They key and respond to our pass rush. Their flanker to our left could be set in the slot between the line unit and center with four receivers in position to flood our right.

FIGURE 14-3 shows the offensive tendencies and possibilities of the "Shotgun." They can run any number of pass patterns coordinating three receivers to one side, and two receivers, to the other side. If they want to effectively run a running play they need to bring the wide flanker or slot into a blocking back position. They can either have the tailback to fake a pass and run, or shovel pass to a flanking back or pulling tight end.

FIGURE 14-4 shows the offensive tendencies and possibilities of the "Swinging gate." If it is a surprise element, it won't take long for defensive players to sense "Panic"; or "Here is what we need to do," on the part of the defensive coach. The term "junk offense" is panic, and the words "Their center is a primary target" are the positive approach. Most of the coaches that we have had to play against in our league, I am sure would use the positive approach.

Tactically, the "swinging gate" system is DARN interesting. It has a passing tailback set 7 to 9 yards behind center with no line for pass blocking to our right. There can be either two or three receivers set in flanking or slot positions to that side. The remaining six linemen on the line-of-scrimmage with a back set behind them are to our left. The back can set to either side of the line unit as a flanker left, or a slot between the unit and center to the right. If he sets to the left it will give them two receivers to our left and three receivers to our right. If he sets in the right slot, it will give them one receiver to our left and four receivers to our right. The center is set to our right when the ball is on that hash mark. If the ball is set on the other hash mark, the formation is totally flip-flopped, with the center to our left, and the line unit to our right.

Their tailback is set to invite a pass rush, and drops back with an order of priorities and options in mind. Both outside receivers go straight down the field. Their right inside receiver hooks with the center cutting off his back to Easy. The left flanker sets up behind his line unit. The tailback has approximately four seconds with his dropback to hit one of his three inside receivers on their primary patterns. The center is his primary target, with the hook man being his secondary receiver. If both of these receivers are covered he hits the left flanker set up behind the line unit. After the four seconds the tailback begins his scramble to the left or right depending on the rush of two defenders. The receivers react on their secondary patterns, with the tailbacks scramble. A mobile screen pass can be run with the line unit to our right, with the left receivers clearing the area out. This can be applied to flip-flop the formation for the following play. All plays can be called at the line of scrimmage without a huddle.

ADJUSTING THE COMBO SYSTEM
TO SPREAD TACTICAL TENDENCIES

The first thing we do is call "Time out," and think 43 prevent defense (Chapter 4). Since they spread our defense out we can count down on their eligible receivers from the inside out, and apply man-to-man keys with zone responsibilities. This is because our basic techniques are always man-to-man regardless of the type of tactical coverage applied, and we can depend on the carry over values from our basic drills (Chapter 6) in making our defensive adjustments.

Against the "Shotgun" our basic 43 prevent defensive adjustments remain basically the same as they would against any other two minute offense. Our two halfbacks key their respective outside receiver and are responsible for Charlie and Able zones. Our safety and split cornerback key their first receivers set from the inside out and apply our zone rotating responsibilities. Our middle linebacker and tight cornerback apply bump and recovery technique on the second receivers set from the outside in forcing them to the inside. They are responsible for Dog and Easy zones respectively. The combo backs up, and covers the hook area in relation to their third inside receiver.

Against the "Swinging gate" we have some adjustments to make with our defensive alignments and keys without any basic changes in our responsibilities, techniques, and reactions. We view their line unit as our tight side, and their tailback and center as our split side. Our tight side end uses his basic set and charges to get a position behind the stationary screen, and is responsible for outside containment of the tailback scramble coming his way. Our split side defensive end rushes the tailback from the backside forcing his scramble towards the tight side. The two tackles shift down into a split, and an inside flanking set on their tight side line unit. The combo backs them up. The middle line backer sets on their tight end, and the tight cornerback sets on their center where they apply their "Bump and recovery" techniques and basic responsibilities. The split cornerback sets in the split between their line unit and center, with basic responsibilities and reactions. The halfbacks and safety key their respective eligible receivers, who are set off the line of scrimmage. They are responsible for their respective zones.

INDIVIDUAL ADJUSTMENTS AGAINST
THE SPREAD FORMATIONS

The individual sets, keys, responsibilities, techniques, and reactions are shown and explained for each position against the "Shotgun" and "Swinging gate" spreads.

FIGURE 14-5 shows the 43 prevent defense against the "Shotgun" spread:

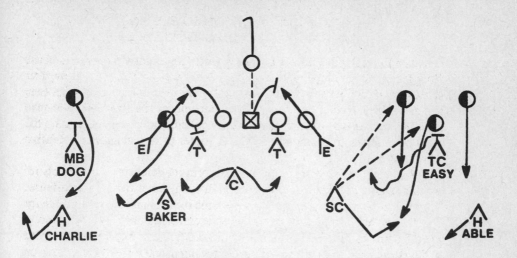

Figure 14-5
43 Prevent Adjustments vs. Shotgun

Left end:

1. SET-Outside and facing through their tight end.
2. KEY-Tailback
3. RESPONSIBILITIES-Pass rush with outside containment.
4. TECHNIQUE-Charge through the set of tight end with an inside shoulder relationship to the tailback.
5. REACTION-Fight through pass blocking to the outside.

Right end:

1. SET-Outside and facing through their offensive tackle.
2. KEY-Tailback
3. RESPONSIBILITIES-Pass rush with outside containment.
4. TECHNIQUE-Charge through the set of their offensive tackle with an inside shoulder relationship to the tailback.
5. REACTION-Fight through the pass blocking to the outside.

Left tackle:

1. SET-On their offensive tackle to our tight side.

2. KEY-Tackle, read his head.
3. RESPONSIBILITIES-Lateral control, both gaps.
4. TECHNIQUE-Forearm shiver, read the head.
5. REACTION-Pass rush.

Combo:

1. SETS-Over the center and off the L.O.S.
2. KEY-Center.
3. RESPONSIBILITIES-Tight side left guard and center gap, hook areas.
4. TECHNIQUE-Play football.
5. REACTION-Back up, both hook areas.

Middle linebacker:

1. SET-On wide flanker to our left. (Second receiver from inside out)
2. KEY-Movement of wide flanker.
3. RESPONSIBILITIES-Outside control forcing the flanker to his inside.
4. TECHNIQUE-Bump and recovery.
5. REACTION-Recover to Dog zone coverage.

Tight cornerback

1. SET-On split end to our right (second receiver from the inside out).
2. KEY-Movement of split end.
3. RESPONSIBILITIES-Outside control forcing the split end to his inside.
4. TECHNIQUE-Bump and recovery.
5. REACTION-Recover to Easy zone coverage.

Split cornerback:

1. SET-Triangle the right split side.
2. KEY-Slot back (First receiver from inside out).
3. RESPONSIBILITIES-Baker zone coverage.
4. TECHNIQUE-Man-to-man.
5. REACTION-Check slotback to hook area and pick up the split end coming into Baker.

Safety:

1. SET-6 to 8 yards off their tight end to our left. (First receiver from inside out).
2. KEY-Movement of tight end.
3. RESPONSIBILITIES-Baker zone, back up hook area.
4. TECHNIQUE-Man-to-man.
5. REACTION-Pick up tight end to Baker.

Left halfback:

1. SET-10 to 12 yards off their wide flanker (outside receiver to our left).
2. KEY-Wide flanker's movement.
3. RESPONSIBILITIES-Charlie zone coverage.
4. TECHNIQUE-Man to man.
5. REACTION-Pick up wide flanker to Charlie.

Right halfback:

1. SET-10 to 12 yards off their wide flanker (Outside receiver to our right).
2. KEY-Wide flanker's movement.
3. RESPONSIBILITIES-Able zone coverage.
4. TECHNIQUE-Man-to-man.
5. REACTION-Pick up wide flanker to Able.

Basically, these defensive adjustments against the "Shotgun" are very similar to those adjustments against a pro-set two minute offense.

FIGURE 14-6 shows the 43 prevent defense against the "Swinging gate" spread:

Left end:

1. SET-Outside, and facing through their tight end set to our left tight side.
2. KEY-The back behind line unit through to their tailback.
3. RESPONSIBILITIES-Stationary screen pass and outside containment of tailback scramble.
4. TECHNIQUE-Charge through the set of tight end.
5. REACTION-Follow through.

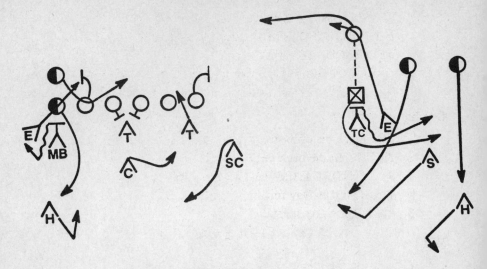

Figure 14-6
43 Prevent Adjustments vs. Swinging Gate

Right end:

1. SET-Outside their center facing the tailback to our right split side.
2. KEY-Tailback.
3. RESPONSIBILITIES-Pass rush with outside shoulder relation to the tailback.
4. TECHNIQUE-Charge and follow through.
5. REACTION-Try to get play from behind.

Left tackle:

1. SET-In the gap in the middle of line unit.
2. KEY-Offensive movement.
3. RESPONSIBILITIES-Penetrate the screen.
4. TECHNIQUE-Quick release.
5. REACTION-Charge through the gap.

Right tackle:

1. SET-On last offensive linemen to the inside of the line unit.

2. KEY-Lineman he is on, read his head.
3. RESPONSIBILITIES-Lateral control at L.O.S.
4. TECHNIQUE-Forearm shiver.
5. REACTION-Inside gap penetrate only after offensive lineman tries to block out.

Combo:

1. SET-Stack his offensive left tackle.
2. KEY-Offensive back behind line unit.
3. RESPONSIBILITIES-Back up line unit.
4. TECHNIQUE-Play football.
5. REACTION-To our right.

Middle linebacker:

1. SET-On their tightside tight end to our left.
2. KEY-Tight end's movement.
3. RESPONSIBILITIES-Force tight end to his inside with Dog zone recovery.
4. TECHNIQUE-Bump and recovery.
5. REACTION-Dog zone coverage.

Tight cornerback:

1. SET-On their split side center to our right.
2. KEY-Center's movement.
3. RESPONSIBILITIES-Force center to his inside, and cover him in Easy flat.
4. TECHNIQUE-Bump and recovery.
5. REACTION-Cover center to Easy flat.

Split cornerback:

1. SET-Triangle split between line unit and center.
2. KEY-Either a slot set in split or tailback.
3. RESPONSIBILITIES-Pick up any one who comes out of their backfield through the split.
4. TECHNIQUE-Man to man.
5. REACTION-Zone.

Safety:

1. SET-6 to 8 yards off the second receiver from inside out to our split side.
2. KEY-Second receiver's movement.
3. RESPONSIBILITIES-Cover him all the way.
4. TECHNIQUE-Man to man.
5. REACTION-Pick him up going to Baker.

Left halfback:

1. SET-10 to 12 yards off the tight side tight end set to our left.
2. KEY-Tight end through to flanker.
3. RESPONSIBILITIES-Charlie zone coverage.
4. TECHNIQUE-Man to man
5. REACTION-Pick up tight end to Charlie.

Right halfback:

1. SET-10 to 12 yards off the outside receiver to the right split side.
2. KEY-Outside flanker.
3. RESPONSIBILITIES-Able zone coverage.
4. TECHNIQUE-Man-to-man.
5. REACTION-Pick up outside flanker to Able.

The "Swinging gate" types of spreads have probably created more defensive tactical adjustments than any other types of offenses. It does not make any difference what an opponent's views are to its tactical consistency; they can not afford to ignore it. Our combo defensive adjustment against the "Swinging gate" type of offense speaks for itself.

Our approach in this chapter has been against the spreads when we might be caught by surprise, without being able to prepare for them during the week before the game. If we already know it is coming we can naturally make more elaborate preparations for it with our game plan.

15

A CONCLUSION FOR THE COMBO DEFENSE

The three phases of football are: Defense, offense, and the kicking game. There are many different viewpoints and opinions among coaches as to which is the most important. We have seen strong offensive teams with weak defenses win, and we have seen strong defensive teams with weak offenses win. They both had one thing in common; and that was a strong kicking game. When a team with both a strong defense and a strong offense loses, it is very often the result of a breakdown in the kicking game. This does not mean that the kicking game is the most important. They all three are important with each being dependent on one another. The phase that requires the most emphasis and work should be the phase that is the weakest.

PROJECTING THE DEFENSIVE POTENTIAL

Sometimes it is difficult to project untested personnel as a team even after a couple of scrimmages in the pre-season practices. The coach can get an over exaggerated opinion of his team's prospects because his offensive unit looked so good. Later in the season he will realize it was not that his offensive unit was that good, but that the defense as a unit was weak. The defense should be ahead of the offense in pre-season, and the offense does not catch-up in progress until the early season. Usually when an untested defensive unit is making the offense look bad in pre-season, this should project encouragement instead of disappointment. We feel if we can have a strong defense along with a good kicking game, we will be able to find ways to score with unproven offensive personnel. The only way a coach can ever be sure in the evaluation of his squad is to have tested all three phases under fire. The pleasant surprises usually appear from the defensive phase than in the other the few disappointments from proven personnel. More "sleepers" who are pleasant surprises usually appear from the defensive phase than in the other two.

DEFENSIVE POINTS-OF-VIEW

Both defensive coaches and their players usually have a broader perspective, and more knowledge about offensive football than the offensive coaches and the players do. As strange as this might seem, it is because the offense is confined to the specialization of their own system. Outside of the quarterback, each player very often carries out assignments by simple rules, and as a result may not realize their total function. Most of the time the changing defenses do not affect their rules. The defense will study and see different offenses from one week to the next. This gives them a much broader viewpoint of offensive football. As a result we very often see defensive players become offensive coaches and students of the offensive game.

DEFENSIVE CHANGES FOLLOW OFFENSIVE INNOVATIONS

The defense must understand the offense before they can effectively stop it. A change in offensive trends will determine the change in the defenses. Coaches are historians. Since offensive innovations are the revival of something old with new wrinkles; coaches study the past to see what defenses were effective against those offenses that have been revived from a particular time. They install those defenses with counter wrinkles. This has been the rotating cycle of tactics. Offensive tactical innovations are usually something old under a new name. Their popularity is simply a result of winning success and exposure. Coaches are very slow to accept a change in their offensive systems: especially if it is very different from what they are familiar with. They find security in only improving their present system. They have a completely different attitude toward their defenses. If they start having tactical problems with their defenses, they will not be nearly as slow about totally accepting another defensive system. As a result the defense has always been trying to keep up with the offense.

REVERSING THE TACTICAL CYCLE

If we reverse our tactical thinking to having a defensive system that is ahead of the changing offenses, then we only have to change our defenses in the frame work of the system. This would tactically put the defenses ahead of the offenses. This would cause us to consider completely changing our offensive systems before we would completely change our defensive systems. How many coaches do you know who really believe, and find more security in their defensive systems, than they do their offensive systems? This thought will make students of the game feel uncomfortable, even though they might feel it is more academic than it is a reality.

THE DIFFERENCE BETWEEN A TACTICAL HEART AND HEAD

What is academic often comes from the heart, and what is reality comes from the head. Basically, our hearts are usually with the offense, and our heads are usually with the defense. We let our hearts overrule our heads, and find more security in the familiarity of our offensive systems than we do our defensive systems.

THE DEFENSIVE AND OFFENSIVE RELATIONSHIP

We usually think in terms of the offense attacking, and the defense stopping the offense. If the defense is going to be aggressive it must also attack. An attacking defense can be turned into an offense. We actually use the same numbering system, zones, and terminology with our combo defensive system that we do with our offensive system. The combo defensive approach can probably be applied with the application of your own numbering system and terminology. This will result in better communications among your staff, and be more meaningful to your players. It can also help a player to make a smooth transformation from the defense to the offense or visa versa.

THE COMMON DENOMINATORS OF THE COMBO SYSTEM

The combo defense is designed to adjust against all the changing offensive tactics within the framework of the system itself. It would be difficult for any coach not to be able to find some of the alignments and techniques of his own defense integrated in part into the combo system. He should also be at least familiar with each of the other combinations applied into the total system. This should motivate his interest, and aid his understanding of the combo defense.

The advantages of the combo defensive system are:

1. It integrates both control and stunt techniques.
2. It is easy for everyone to understand.
3. It is flexible enough to adjust against all the different offensive systems without creating new learning situations for the defensive players.
4. It is natural in using drills with carry over values for the system.
5. It prevents player hesitation, and being caught out of position.
6. It maintains interest because of variations beyond the repetition of techniques.
7. It maintains communication between the defensive and offensive players and staff.
8. It creates confidence and a challenge among the defensive players.
9. It can be adjusted in the spur of the moment against tactical surprises.

Defensive coaches must be familiar with every type of offense that is in use. The combo system can be adjusted against any type of offense that you might run into, and you should be able to find it within these pages. You might have to prepare against an unbalanced slot T offense, such as we have in our league, and think that it has not been covered in this book. Basically apply the secondary adjustments in Chapter 8 along with defensive front alignments in Chapter 13 against an unbalanced Slot T. With knowledge of the contents that have been presented here, and your own initiative, you should be able to make defensive adjustment against any variation in offensive systems using the combo system. The glossary which follows will serve you as a point of reference.

GLOSSARY

Able Zone - The right deep third of the defensive secondary.

Adjustments - Defensive sets through reaction to counter alignments in offensive formations.

Agility - A degree of balance between speed and control.

Agility Drills - Physical repetition to improve agility skills.

Alignments - Sets of the unit or team as a whole.

Backfield Techniques - The elements used in putting basic backfield maneuvers into action.

Backside Calls When the backfield is set strong from the point of attack.

Backside Series - When the play or sequence is run from the side the wingback is set.

Baker Zone - The middle deep third of the defensive secondary.

Balanced Line - When there are three men on the line of scrimmage to each side of center.

Belly Series - The three play option sequence based on a fake ride of the fullback.

Blocking Back - Is set immediately behind his offensive line to be utilized for trapping or sealing the hole.

Blocking Rules - The system for basic types of blocking assignments.

Blocking Terms - The basic words that are used in the integration of the basic blocking rules.

Bootleg - A term to designate a pass or run sequence to the backside.

Break Drill - Physical repetition for pass defenders to improve their skills of judging and reacting to the ball while it is in the air.

Buck Lateral - A term to describe a four play running sequence run from a single wing.

Bump And Recovery - A defensive technique used on an eligible receiver immediately after the snap.

Call - The signal that designates a play or set.

Call Man - The lead blocker to the inside of the hole that is designated by the digit in the call.

Charlie Zone - The left deep third of the defensive secondary.

Check And Release - A technique for backside offensive linemen to force defensive players to their outside shoulders before going downfield to block.

Clear Out - When a primary receiver takes his front line defenders to a deep zone leaving the short zone open for a secondary receiver.

Comeback Drill - Physical repetition for pass defenders to improve their skills against the hook pass.

Combo - A term for a combination of components from different defenses to make a single defense.

Combo System - The rules and principles for the combo defense.

Corner Back - The linebackers outside of ends off the line of scrimmage.

Counter - Misdirection play away from backfield pattern.

Cross Block - A blocking maneuver at the point of attack where an outside offensive lineman blocks down, and an inside lineman blocks out.

Covered Linemen - Offensive interior linemen with a defensive down lineman on them.

Cut Back - A maneuver by a ball carrier when he turns head on against the defensive pursuit.

Cut Off - A blocking term for an offensive lineman who applies a technique to fill the hole to his inside that was left by a pulling lineman.

Day Light - An opening for a ball carrier in the defensive front.

Defensive Tendencies - Based on the strong and weak characteristics of the defense or offense.

Delay - A count hesitation applied by the uncovered interior linemen and backs.

Deployment - Shifting offensive players from their basic positions to a secondary set.

Dog Zone - The left short half of the defensive secondary.

Double Team - A general term that can either be applied to tandem or post and lead blocking. It can also be applied to two on one situations such as the option.

Double Wing - Formations with any combination of either slots or flanker to both sides and only one running back.

Draw - Delayed running plays following a fake dropback pass.

Drills - Physical repetition to improve skills.

Drop Back - The basic backfield maneuver for a passing attack.

Eagle Defense - The 53 defense that originated against the "Bear T."

Easy Zone - The right short half of the defensive secondary.

Even Defense - Has an uncovered center.

Even Gaps - The digits in the call that indicate the holes to the right through which the defensive front stunts.

Even Holes - The digits in the call that indicate the points of attack to the right for ball carriers.

Exterior - The term for the outside containment units of the defense.

Exterior Gaps - The 4, 5, 6, and 7 calls which designate the stunts of the defensive ends and cornerbacks.

Exterior Sets - Alignments for the defensive ends and cornerbacks.

Exterior Stunts - Variations of gap responsibilities between a defensive end and cornerback to one side.

Finesse - One of three tactical characteristics which puts emphasis on consistent execution.

Flanker - A secondary frontside set for the wing back to the outside of his end.

Flat - The outside areas of the short zones.

Flip-Flop - Either linemen or backs to exchange the set of their basic positions from one side to the other.

Floater - The secondary frontside set for a wingback either as a slot or flanker.

Forearm Shiver - A contact technique that a defensive lineman used to get control of an offensive lineman.

Formation - The set of all the offensive players.

Frontside Calls - When the backfield is set strong to the point of attack.

Frontside Series - When the play or sequence is run to the side the wingback is set.

Fullhouse Backfield Set - When all three running backs are set in their basic positions.

Game Plan - A tactical format based on opponents' tendencies.

Gap - A defensive hole between two offensive players.

Goal Line Defense - Short yardage defenses. (83 and 65 calls)

Halfbacks - The left and right defensive secondary positions that are responsibile for the outside deep 1/3s (Charlie and Able zones) of the field.

Hashmark Drill - Physical repetition for pass defenders to improve their skills of maintaining good position, and covers two receivers in one zone.

Hole - Offensive point of attack.

Hook - A short inside pass pattern.

Hook Area - The inside of the short zones.

Influence - An offensive maneuver to give a false key to lead a defensive player from the play.

Inside Linebacker - Any linebackers set between our two defensive tackles.

Inside Gap - A frontside blocking term used in all blocking rules, or relationships of defensive down linemen.

Interior - The term for the inside unit of the defensive front.

Interior Gaps - The 0, 1, 2, and 3 calls which designate the stunts for the combo, middle linebacker and tackles.

Interior Sets - Alignments for both tackles, the combo, and the middle linebacker.

Invert Rotation - A defensive maneuver by two inside defensive backs adjusting to sets or backfield flow.

Isolation (ISO) A blocking rule and technique.

Jab Step - A quick lead step with delay.

Key - Second step in a defensive assignment.

Keying - Watching an assigned opponent to determine set and reaction.

Lead Block - A term and technique done by the call man who blocks the first defensive man to the inside of the hole or off the L.O.S.

L.O.S. - Line of scrimmage.

Man In Motion - One offensive back moving laterally with the L.O.S. before the snap.

Man-To-Man - Matching up players in defensive coverage. (Basic technique)

Mirror Drill - Physical repetition to improve the skill of open field position and control.

Middle Linebacker - The interior linebacker for the combo defense.

Monster - A roving defensive linebacker playing the strongside of the offense.

Multiple Elements - Many integrated techniques and formations.

N.L.B. - Near linebacker closest to point of attack.

Non-Rhythm Count - A delay between each phase of the snap signal to prevent mistakes because of anticipation.

Odd Defense - Has a covered center.

Odd Gaps - The digits in the call that indicate the holes to the left through which the defensive front stunts.

Odd Holes - The digit in the call that indicates the point of attack to the left for ball carriers.

On - A defensive down lineman set directly in front of an offensive lineman on the L.O.S.

One On One Drill - Physical repetition to improve the skill in man-to-man techniques.

Option - An offensive maneuver to put two offensive men on one defensive man, and then making a choice.

Outside Gap - A backside blocking term, or a defensive set with an outside shoulder relationship to offensive lineman.

Overshifted - A term applied to the defense when they have shifted down one full man against an unbalanced line, or offensive set.

Passing Tree - All the pass patterns and calls for an individual receiver set in a certain position.

Patterns - The route for a receiver on a single pass pattern.

Pitch Out - Lateral the ball to another player.

Phases Of The Game - Offensive, defensive, and kicking games.

Pivot - The technique of an individual turning on the ball of his jab foot before his execution.

Platoon - A term applied to specialized programing of two teams for two phases.

Playaction - A term to designate the pattern of the backfield.

Play The Game - The short yardage offense, vs. the short yardage defense.

Plotting Tendencies - Establishing patterns of a team's characteristics.

Pocket - Pass blockers in a concave set in the backfield for pass protection.

Point Of Attack - The hole in the line designated by the second digit of the call.

Post And Lead Block - A term and technique in rules that applies to the first offensive linemen to the inside of the call man in a double team situation.

Power - One of three tactical characteristics that puts emphasis on strength.

Power Rules - A basic type of blocking assignment for offensive plays.

Power Techniques - Used by the backfield and offensive line.

Pre-Snap - Before the ball is centered to start the play.

Prevent - A 43 defense that sacrifices short yardage for a touchdown, and to run time out on the clock.

Primary Targets - The first in choice of two pass receivers working on one defender.

Priority - An order for a running sequence, pass patterns, or defensive assignments.

Program - A long range format for consistency in producing good teams.

Pro Set - A formation with a wide flanker and tight end to one side, a split end to the other, and two running backs.

Pro 43 - A 4-3-4 defensive alignment use against the pro set.

Pull Or Puller - Applies to an offensive interior lineman who pulls behind his own line to trap or seal.

Pump - A fake action with the passing arm.

Pursuit - A reaction angle of defensive players to keep the ball carrier between them and the sideline past the line of scrimmage.

Reach - Both an offensive and defensive term applied to a lineman assigned to make contact on his adjacent lineman's opponent.

Reaction - The fifth step in a defensive assignment.

Reaction Drill - Physical repetition to improve skills in reacting to movement of the ball.

Reading - Anticipating the opponent's team maneuvers through individual keys.

Responsibilities - The third step in a defensive assignment.

Reverse - The third play in series to the backside that is applied after a playaction fake.

Reverse Pivot - To lead from the call making a full turn in one motion before execution.

Safety - A defensive secondary position responsible for the middle deep 1/3 (Baker zone) of the field.

Safety Blitz - A safety stunt where he is called to shoot a gap.

Scoop Drill - Physical repetition to improve the skill of picking up a fumble on the run.

Scouting Reports - A tactical and personnel evaluation of another team.

Scramble - A follow up blocking technique.

Seal Block - A blocking term for the first man outside the hole to block the first inside defensive man off the line of scrimmage.

Secondary - The defensive backfield.

Secondary Target - The second in choice of pass receivers.

Sequence - A backfield pattern where all plays look alike, and their only difference is in who gets the ball.

Series - The first digits in the call that indicate the sequence and sets.

Set - The secondary position before the snap, or the first step in a defensive assignment.

Set Adjustments - Changing the defensive positions before the snap to counter the offensive formations.

Shift - Used by the backfield to get from their basic position to a secondary set before the snap.

Shiver Drill - Physical repetition for a defensive lineman improving his technique of getting forearm control on an offensive lineman.

Short Punt - A supplementary offensive formation that was used with the single wing. It used a cross spinner and trap sequence.

Shortside - To the weakside of an unbalanced line.

Shotgun - A balanced spread formation with five flanking eligible receivers, and the passer already set deep.

Shovel Pass - A play where a deep tailback pitches the ball forward to a back close behind trap blocking at the L.O.S.

Signal - Calls at the line-of-scrimmage to designate the snap.

Single Wing - A very popular offense perfected during the 20's and 30's. The formations did not have a quarterback under center, and it required a direct snap to the fullback or tailback. It was run behind both balanced and unbalanced lines and featured double team blocking.

Slant - A backfield technique used in sequence where the halfback takes a hand off over tackle usually after a fake.

Slot - A secondary set for the wingback between his split end and tackle.

Slot I - Formation set behind a split end and slot back to the frontside, and a tight end to the backside.

Snap - Putting the ball into play at the line of scrimmage.

Snap Drill - Physical repetition of a defensive player getting off the ball on movement.

Specialization - A player concentrating on but one phase of the game.

Speed - One of three tactical characteristics that puts emphasis on quickness.

Spinner - A backfield maneuver from the single wing or short punt.

Split Cornerback - The outside linebacker set in a triangle of the slot to the split side.

Split End - Offensive end who spreads wide on L.O.S.

Split Side - The side to which the offensive end is split leaving only two tight adjacent linemen between him and the center.

Split 44 - A technique type of defensive front.

Split "T" - A very popular offense that was developed during the 40's.

Sprintback - A term to designate a pass from a sweep backfield action using a fourth receiver without a fake.

Stack - A defensive linebacker set directly behind his down lineman.

Stack 44 - A stunting type of defensive front.

Stair Case - A pass pattern in which the receiver runs a square cut to the flat, and then cuts straight up the field when the quarterback pumps.

Statue Of Liberty - The classical fake pass and wide reverse.

Statistics - Test and measurements of a team's history.

Strategy - A tactical plan of attack.

Strongside - To the long side of the unbalanced line, or the offensive flanker's side.

Stunt - Shooting an assigned gap while basic responsibilities are being covered by another player.

Sweep - A play using pulling guards and a flanker to get wide.

Sweep Rules - A basic type of blocking rules used with sweep and slant plays.

Sweep Techniques - Used by the backfield to get wide.

Swinging Gate - An overshifted spread formation with three or four receivers to one side, and one or two to the other.

System - Tactical methods.

Tactical Cycle - The continuous revival of tactical football from emphasis on speed to power and back to speed again.

Tactical Tendencies - The characteristics and relationships between an individual team's tactics and personnel.

Tandem - A double team blocking technique used by two backs to the outside of the hole.

Tandem Rules - A basic type of blocking assignment to double team and isolate at the hole.

Targets - Two pass receivers working on one defender.

Techniques - Method of execution. The fourth step in a defensive assignment.

Tight Cornerback - The outside linebacker set on their tight end.

Tight End - Offensive end who is set close to his adjacent offensive tackle on the L.O.S.

Tight Side - The side to which the offensive end is closed down leaving three tight adjacent offensive linemen to the one side of center.

Tip Drill - Physical repetition for pass defenders in the skills of pass interceptions.

Trap - A blocking maneuver to take a defensive player out after he was allowed to penetrate the hole.

Triad - A single technique or term being applied to three sets of blocking rules.

Tripe-Option - The quarterback and fullback two on one the defensive tackle with the belly option. Then the quarterback options the keep or pitches off the defensive end.

Veer - Running the triple option sequence from a split backfield behind a pro set line.

Unbalanced Line - When there are four men on the line of scrimmage to one side of center and two to the other side.

Uncovered Linemen - Offensive interior linemen with no defensive down linemen on them.

Undershifted - When the defensive interior line makes no adjustment to an unbalanced line.

Walk Away - A set adjustment of defensive ends to the split side of a balanced line or the shortside of an unbalanced line.

Wave Drill - Physical repetition to improve body control in reaction to the movement of the ball.

Weave Drill - Physical repetition for pass defenders to use cross over steps without turning their backs on the ball.

Wingback - The name of the position. His secondary sets could be flanker or slot.

Winged "T" - Offenses developed during the 50's that combined singlewing blocking with "T" backfield techniques.

Wishbone Formation - The current set from which the triple option is run.

Zone - The five areas into which the defensive secondary is divided.

Zone Coverage - An area type of defensive coverage.

INDEX